Prayers for Worship Leaders

PRAYERS
for
WORSHIP LEADERS

Arnold Kenseth and *Richard P. Unsworth*

FORTRESS PRESS   PHILADELPHIA

COPYRIGHT © 1978 BY FORTRESS PRESS

Third Printing 1983

———

Library of Congress Cataloging in Publication Data

Kenseth, Arnold.
  Prayers for worship leaders.

  1. Prayers. I. Unsworth, Richard P., joint
author.   II. Title.
BV250.K46   248'.8   77-15249
ISBN 0-8006-1331-7

———

688K83   Printed in the United States of America 1-1331

To
Samuel H. Miller
and to
Molly Miller
for friendship and grace

Petitions

It is into our prayers pour our fatigues, gasps
After your ear. O Radiance, hear us. Hold,
And let our cries come. Our fluttering grasps
For your branches. May we be so bold?
Under our knees earth rocks. Rage is in it.
There are alarms, rumors. Miscreants wander.
Rhetorics, riots. Our white houses founder.
Miserable, we creep into your turret.

O is it that our tongues, brassy and gonging
In time's gossip, unbell in the burning?
How to sound you for the terror churning
In us? What speech for cancer, frigidity, rue?
Words shrivel. Groan is all, and all is longing.
O catch our gestures, Vast; and make them true.

ARNOLD KENSETH

Contents

Preface

This book arose out of a "concern," in the Quaker meaning of that word. As persons charged with responsibility for public worship—one of us a parish minister, the other a college chaplain—we have had frequent occasion to scour the sources. As clergy in the Reformed tradition, we are accustomed to writing prayers suitable for particular occasions and circumstances, and to drawing freely upon the treasury of Christian prayers that has accumulated in official prayer books and unofficial collections of prayers.

In recent years we have become aware of an increasing difficulty in finding published prayers that commend themselves readily for public worship. The classical collections, both official and unofficial, are cast in King James English, consonant with the Authorized Version so long in common use in public worship. In the past two decades congregations have become increasingly acclimated to vernacular translations of the Bible—the Revised Standard Version, the New English Bible, and the Jerusalem Bible—and to contemporary usage in the language of public prayers. During the same period there have been a number of revisions of standard prayer books, some more felicitous than others, and countless small collections of prayers for private use. It has been our impression that some of the former and most of the latter have failed to measure up to the simple canons of good English—economy, clarity, and a pointed choice of words.

The language of prayer should have additional marks. It should touch and recall ordinary human experience, but it should do so in a way that reflects God's glory. "Ordinary" must never mean "banal," for prayer elevates our human experience to be examined in the light of divine grace. In that light our needs and situations, our responsibilities and hopes are shown up as the targets of God's love and the objects of an empowering Spirit. The language of prayer, then, ought to be spacious and imaginative, earthy, evocative, illuminating. It need not be ornate. In fact, it *should* not be. But neither need it be chatty and didactic. Of all the modes of language, it ought to be among the most realistic, which is to say that it ought to be a fit vehicle for lifting the reality of who we are into the reality of God's provident presence.

The prayers in this volume have been composed with such criteria in mind. They were written for specific occasions and used by worshiping congregations. They are the product of public worship whose participants have included tradespeople, students, professional men and women, children, academics, farmers, and artisans. We offer them for publication not audaciously but hopefully, reckoning that we should risk adding what we can to the resources available to clergy and laity who look—as we often do—for published prayers that either speak to situations in public worship or suggest how one might speak to such situations.

While this collection is organized around the needs of public worship, we are very dubious about any sharp lines that delineate public from private prayer. It has been our own experience, at least, that prayer finally leads us to the discovery of our common humanity, and therefore that prayers best suited for public use are often those best suited for private utterance as well.

It was Ralph Waldo Emerson who said that "a foolish consistency is the hobgoblin of little minds." So, let us claim large-mindedness rather than irresponsibility to explain the liberties we have taken with consistent form. We have not, for example, edited every prayer to achieve a uniform contemporary usage. Some prayers, first written in King James English, have been left in their original form, especially where a change would alter the essential structure of the prayer. Those who are committed to contemporary usage only should be able, if they please, to adapt an occasional King Jamesism without difficulty.

We have also avoided rigid criteria to govern the gender of pronouns referring to the Divine Person. It is our conviction that, in this as in other questions of language, usage creates rules as much as it follows them. And while the growing sensitivity to implicit and explicit sexism in the language of the church is legitimate and beneficial, the fact remains that usage hasn't yet sorted itself out, and probably won't for some years to come. Another consideration: surely God is not male, but equally surely God encompasses rather than escapes our human differentiations, sexual and otherwise. Thus we have not hesitated to use gendered pronouns where it has seemed appropriate, particularly in the case of biblical quotations that would jar the sensibilities if tampered with, even in the name of an essentially proper concern about sexism.

A word should be said about the structure of this collection. It is organized in the expectation that it will be used in public worship, but also in the recognition that worship is public as often outside the walls of a church as within them.

The sections on the liturgy and the Christian year

are aimed chiefly at those offices that take place in the sanctuary. The prayers for the liturgy follow the familiar architecture of liturgy in the Reformed tradition, and include prayers of invocation, adoration and praise, confession, thanksgiving, intercession, and petition. The benedictions included are those less likely to be in the memory of every liturgist. There are also prayers to be used on occasions when the Lord's Supper is celebrated. As will be obvious, these are not designed to replace but to supplement the Great Prayer, or Prayer of Consecration, that is provided in the prayer books of the church.

Awareness of the Christian year has been less pronounced in those churches with roots in the Anabaptist and Reformed traditions than among Episcopalian, Lutheran, Orthodox, and Catholic churches. One who paid too much attention to the liturgical year in a New England Congregational church would have been branded, not many decades ago, as a "papist." So the rich appeal to imagination and the great teaching value of the Christian year were all too often lost to Christians in these less liturgically oriented communions.

One great practical contribution of the ecumenical movement to Protestant spirituality has been the recovery of the resources of the Christian year for our common worship. Lectionaries are more often followed, as evidenced by the largely successful attempts to coordinate the lectionaries of the major Christian churches. And it has been our recent experience, in this New England fastness, that young and old alike show a heightened appreciation of the seasonal character of Christian worship. In our section on the Christian year, we have tried to reflect this development. We have not attempted to cover the whole liturgical calendar, but we have tried to provide amply for the major seasons of Advent, Lent, and Holy Week, as well

14

as for the major days: Christmas, Epiphany, Easter, Pentecost, and All Saints. We have presented this part of the collection with a special conviction that what once emerged as a great device for Christian pedagogy is as necessary now as it ever was. In fact, it would not be hard to prove that biblical illiteracy is more rampant now than ever. In any event, the religious imagination needs what the Christian year can furnish.

The second half of this book is devoted to prayers for special occasions and prayers for special needs and persons. These prayers have all been written for public worship, those for special needs and persons being occasional prayers that have been composed as part of the pastoral prayer in Sunday liturgies.

The prayers for special occasions reflect our understanding that prayer is still public wherever two or three are gathered in Christ's name, whether that be a hospital room, a family dinner table, a baptism at home, a public park on Memorial Day, or an assembly hall at the opening of a school year. If "public worship" encompasses all occasions of corporate prayer both inside and outside the church, the types of occasion are numberless. We have tried to anticipate some of those where the Christian is called upon to officiate as a leader of public prayer. Thus we have included prayers composed for both religious and civil occasions.

In sharing prayers we have written for special needs and persons, we have offered those which touch on the intercessory needs that most often present themselves. In many ways this has been the most difficult section to prepare. In the nature of the case these prayers have been composed with unique events and particular personal situations in mind. Some are phrased in more general language than others, but there is about most of them a concreteness and particularity which may make them less transferable to another circumstance.

So we expect that they may be helpful chiefly by their suggestiveness, as models or images that may evoke the reader's own utterances on behalf of similar needs and persons in one's own worshiping congregation.

Much of the art of public prayer is that of presenting the particular in such a way that it exposes at least one thread of the fabric of human experience. For example, prayers composed for a funeral dare not be so general as to obscure the particular quality of one person's life, nor dare they be personal in an idiosyncratic or subjective way. What is inescapably true of the prayers in a funeral service ought to be true of all prayers used in public worship. They ought to expose the whole tissue of connections that bind us to God and to one another, and they ought to do so one filament at a time. In that way prayer ought to imitate the Incarnation, God's chosen speech for addressing us. That Word was at once encompassing and particular, corporate and personal. The words of prayer can never be as much, but they can be crafted after such a model.

RICHARD P. UNSWORTH

Prayers for Worship Leaders

PRAYERS FOR THE LITURGY

Invocation

Engage us, O Lord, among all the signs, visible and invisible, which discover thy presence among us, so that, illuminated by thy grace, we shall enter into each day's circumstance empty of our pretensions, unafraid of our fears, and alert to every new possibility. As you intend us to be open to all the seasons of the soul, empower us to give of our heart's love generously to all who need us. Help us to honor the goodness in others, and keep us faithful to every thought and act that works against the evil one; through Christ our Lord. Amen.

* * *

O Eternal God, in whose law we find our guidance, in whose love we find our healing and our joy, in whose will we find our goal: do thou so rule over our spirits in this hour that we will go from our worship with the freedom of those whose trust is in thee and who need have no more anxiety for themselves. Teach us to take our delight in thee, to stay our pride in what we own and what we have done, and to count the doing of thy will to be our only glory. We ask this in the name of Jesus Christ our Lord, in whom we see true humility and obedience. Amen.

Invocation

O God of light eternal, in whose love and power the world took shape, and we were born, and our lives are lived, and we die: grant us now that silence of the heart in which we can recall that we are never separated from the love which created us, nor from the love that surrounds our suffering. Bring us now into thy presence, and let us be strengthened there. Amen.

* * *

Come, Sovereign Lord, and awaken in us those needs of flesh and soul, of loss and hope, of wound and healing which we must cry out before thee, for our own sakes and for the sake of all peoples. Be that leaping grace, that generosity of spirit by which we care anew for what happens to the human race. Make us sensible to the ache and anxiety in the world and open to the cries for help. Let our prayers shape what we will do to mend, overcome, and make new. And Christ be with us all. Amen.

Invocation

Come, Holy Spirit, into the prayers we cry out for the sake of all peoples, for their healing and for their salvation. Overcome our little faith and empower both our words and our silences with that love that loves without anxiety. Brood and sigh in us the grievances and sorrows, the ache and the loneliness of all those near and far away who need our intercessions. Take us out of ourselves and into their need. Give us the trust which knows that, beyond our asking is thyself— gathering, comforting, and healing. Amen.

* * *

Gentle Lord, find in us this day whatever desires to handle life with a joyous desire. Put our arms around the sad ones that they may be comforted. Let our eyes love the unloved ones that they may become again part of the human family. Give into our hands the healing touch whereby fevers cool, brokenness mends, fears vanish away. And in thy name help us to take ourselves and others through the dark passages of death in the sure hope of a high and holy resurrection; through Christ our Lord. Amen.

Adoration and Praise

Praise to our Lord God who, in the beginning, sends forth the light over all that is, as well as airs that give breath to the peoples who stand or run on the earth. Praise to our Lord God who arises before us and keeps in love the days of our lives, who holds also by a great tenderness the sadness of the cities and the works of the nations. Praise to our Lord God who intends us for rejoicing in his presence and therefore teaches us ways of compassion to overcome evil and gestures of trust to disarm fear. Praise to our Lord God who makes death to die and gathers everyone at last into paradises no one can name. Praise to our Lord God! Amen.

* * *

Praise the Lord, our God who is everywhere yet has no place, our God who carries time as a very little thing yet who fulfills all time, our God who allows motion and chaos and varieties beyond name yet who so manages that the universe abides. Praise the Lord, our God who sends the snows and the melting rains and the awakening spring, the long sun of summer, fires in the clamorous fall, our God who permits our histories, our God who summons the nations. Praise the Lord, our God who intends us, informs us, and sustains us forever. Amen.

Adoration and Praise

Let us be glad in the ways of the Lord who presides among stars yet teaches the human heart, who gives the seasons that both flesh and nations shall know their sad mortalities, who authors the mystery of our freedom and risks the divine love among our human choices, who intends that each one shall go without fear and that all shall share the music of the deep heavens, who gathers us to learn together who we are in the presence of the Most High. Let us be glad and truly rejoice in the ways of the Lord who is our health and our salvation. Amen.

* * *

Praised be our Lord God who daylight by daylight provides us airs for breathing, skies for dreaming, and sceneries of small streams and fields with many birds to teach the eyes. Praised be our Lord God who has set us now among the great colors of the seasons wherefore we may inwardly dance among any troubles and outwardly rejoice in the new sun. Praised be our Lord God who has given us much always of compassion for our daily ills, a solace that he intends us to give also to others. Praised be our Lord who saves us at the hour of our death, a mysterious happening which is the nature of his love. Praise! Praise! Praise! Amen.

Adoration and Praise

Holy, holy, holy is the visible world and the children who walk and run upon it, and they who speak in the morning airs, and they who, lifting up their eyes, behold the sun's journey and hold out their hands to the rain's fall. Blessed before all is the Lord who, out of mysteries and divine imaginings, spins in the dark and reaching spaces this earth whose rivers wander and roll to the seas, whose valleys sound and resound with great silences, whose mountains are the mountains of rejoicing, whose hills are the hills of hope. It is the Lord who awakens us, who gives us this day and this season. Amen, amen, and amen.

* * *

How good it is to praise you, O elusive One, you strider down the other side of heaven, you in our kitchens, you now under the green trees turning toward the autumn! May our breath praise you as we sigh; may this gesture and that in love and hope praise you; may our tears for others praise you; may our loneliness praise you; may our listening praise you . . . world without end. Amen.

Confession

Sovereign Lord, thy righteousness over us, thy goodness before us, and thy love among us magnify the thousand ways, blatant and devious, we have wasted our lives on that which does not satisfy. We admit sadly that we have too often given our substance and our purpose to capture the mirage and our affections to the things which perish. So we cry pardon for our idolatries and mercy upon our frailties, desiring in our hearts to know those holy, true ways by which the days of our lives shall deepen down in the wellsprings, the unsullied grace, the original joy; through Christ our Lord. Amen.

* * *

Lord, who neither betrays nor condemns and who desires in us only a loving heart: we have been traitorous toward thee and turned each to our own way; we have been quick to judge and slow to forgive; we have given of ourselves cautiously. So we yield to treacheries small and great, settle for trivia, and embrace shadows; so we cry our need. Open to us your always new way where, with patience and hope, we may trust the world to your governance and turn our faces once more toward your holy mysteries that renew all things in every hour. Amen.

Confession

Keeper of the universe, Creator of life, Guardian of our deaths: one and all, we have raged against the heavens, wasted our substance and the gifts given, feared our mortality. Avoiding timelessness, we have become enslaved to time. Careless with means, we go corrupt toward ends. Strangers before death, we are not at home with life. Therefore, great Lord, recall us to the majesties beyond our words, and turn us again to handle with awe the lively world we did not earn; through Jesus Christ who has dominion over death. Amen.

* * *

Lord of all souls everywhere and in all times, we admit to sins, great and small, obvious and subtle, by which we destroy others—those near and dear to us, the peoples far away, the neighbor close by, the stranger in our midst. We acquire rather than share, demand rather than give, avenge rather than pardon. We put other gods before you and learn to live comfortably with what is meaningless and false. As we are ashamed, pity us; as we are aware, strengthen us; as we see through the idolatries, forgive us. Return us to yourself that we may live without fear and seize our days with exultation. Amen.

Confession

Almighty God, whom we are called to love with our whole heart, mind, soul, and with a bold strength: we know well that we are often heartless toward the misery of others and mindless toward thy purposes for good, that our souls wither among our machines, that our strength has gone from us laboring after that which does not satisfy. By our luxury the hungry are sent empty away; for the sake of our comfort the innocent perish at home and abroad. As of old, we kill the prophets and anoint the fools. Help us, great Lord, to deplore in ourselves the evil that so wantonly destroys; and provoke in us for the sake of all people those inward changes which support life, encourage liberty, and make possible the pursuit of happiness. Amen.

* * *

Most gracious Lord, we confess that in ways devious and hardhearted we have worked against thy purposes for an open and loving world. We have profited at the expense of the poor and glossed over the immoralities of the marketplace. We have claimed special rights and privileges which we have denied others. We have forgotten history. Surely we have need of a great repentance. Therefore we beseech thy pardon and the blowing of thy Spirit through our lives that we may be set free from our bondage to greed and live our days with understanding hearts. Amen.

Confession

Lord God, whose mercy is everlasting and whose love surpasses our understanding: we confess that we have been uncertain and faithless servants. We have set our hearts on our own comforts and have ignored the burdens that others carry. We have seen our brothers and sisters hungry or hurt or poor or lonely and have not tried to help them. We have grown patient with injustice and tolerant of war, so long as we have not been their victims. We are sorry for our callousness, and pray for new hearts to see our neighbors' needs and new strength to meet them; through Jesus Christ our Lord. Amen.

* * *

O wondrous Hope, God of the promise, on whom we rely for life and its meaning: we confess that we have sinned against you by abandoning hope, by failing to hear or accept your promises, by relying on ourselves to be both the source and the object of our own faith. Forgive us, we pray, and once more open our hearts to your mercy, our minds to your promise, our hands to our neighbor in need. Restore us to faith in your providing care and your guiding love; through Jesus Christ our Lord. Amen.

Confession

Eternal God, we confess that we have praised you with our lips but have not glorified you with our lives. Have mercy on us, we pray, for our brief faith that fades under pressure, for our quick enthusiasms that just as quickly die, for the hopes we proclaim but do not pursue. Forgive us, Lord God, and give us new trust in your power, that we may live for justice and tell of your loving-kindness by our acts as by our words; through Jesus Christ our Lord. Amen.

* * *

Lord God, we confess that we are not ready for your kingdom of love and peace to be established among us. We still turn away from others' suffering; we still postpone caring for your gift of creation; we still tolerate war and take too lightly the burdens of making peace. Forgive us, O God, for our unreadiness. Awaken us once more to your presence among us, and make of us signs of the coming victory of your mercy; through Jesus Christ, the child of your love and the brother to our hopes. Amen.

Thanksgiving

For the new day and its visible weathers that teach our flesh and alert us to the stretch and pause of the very universe, we give thee thanks, O God. For the morning which has broken our darkness both without and within and opened us to the new possibilities, we give thee thanks, O God. For the day's procession, its landscapes, varieties, intentions, tastes, silences, and dreams, we give thee thanks, O God. For thyself touching, anguishing, persuading, exposing our very being into life and life eternal, we give thee thanks now and forever. Amen. Amen. Amen.

* * *

O Lord our God, whose beauty is everywhere around us on such a morning, whose holiness lays hold of our hearts and minds through what we see: we give wholehearted thanks for the joys of this life, asking only that we be permitted to remember them when darker moments come and your promising presence is shadowed. We are grateful for the ties of love in our families, for the roots and tendrils that have fed our freedom, for the tensions and disagreements that have made us measure our accountability, for the caring circle within whose safety we are called to grow in faith in you and love for one another. Amen.

Thanksgiving

O Most High, from whose bounty we are fed, by whose hand we are guided, and by whose love we are renewed every day: grant us a thankful spirit for all the blessings we know and use—for food enough and to spare, for shelter and the comfort of our quarters, for the gift of reason and the bonds of love. May we never take for granted these supports of daily life, given to us out of the vastness of your love, and granted with the expectation that we will be good stewards of what we have. Amen.

* * *

Generous Lord, who brings us again to the summer dreaming, who unlooses us in the green pastures and beside the still waters, who allows us the lolling sun for a season and lends us the miracle of trees: find in us now a rejoicing among the tastes and the sounds, the flights and the returnings, and encourage in us those gestures of the mind and flesh whereby, over and over, we make of the hours a thanksgiving and of the years a constant praise. Amen.

Thanksgiving

Gracious Lord God, whose glory is nowhere more visible than on our own landscape now, whose earth cannot help but praise you both in its living and in its dying: hear our prayers of thanksgiving. We remember with gratitude the many daily blessings that sustain us:
   —a letter in the morning mail
   —a conversation that got somewhere
   —an idea that struck fire in our imagination
   —the fact that we did not have to worry whether
      there would be food on our tables
   —the fact that no bombs dropped on our village
      today.
O God, by your love and your mercy may it be that all our brothers and sisters everywhere will be able to give thanks for gifts like these. Amen.

* * *

Gracious Lord God, by whom our roots are nourished and our life is sustained, we praise your name for your presence that never fails, even when we have failed you. We give thanks that by your love we know love and are able to love; that by your justice we are able to know what justice requires of us; that by your peace we learn what we must do to be peacemakers; that by your forgiveness we know both how to give and how to receive the forgiveness that can bind up this world's wounds and heal our divisions. Confirm in us a never-failing trust in your love, your justice, your peace, and your forgiveness; through Jesus Christ our Lord. Amen.

Thanksgiving

O Lord our God, hear our prayer of wonder and thanks for all the bounty which is ours to sustain life and adorn it—an abundance of food, comfort in our homes, friendships and duties, failures that have humbled us and successes that have reassured us. Preserve us, we pray, from losing our sense of wonder and gratitude for all that we have, and from being ungenerous toward those who have little goods and great needs. Bind us to the company of men and women throughout time whose thankfulness has kept alive their charity. Amen.

* * *

O God, we praise thee and thank thee for thyself who takes an acorn and makes it a tree, sets air over us and daylight and the large pictures of each season, gives us the walk and run of the body, the mind's radar, and the heart's insatiable dreams. We praise thee and thank thee for thyself who gives us the gifts we do not earn and the strength we do not have and the forgiveness we do not deserve. Unto thee be all glory and honor, dominion and power, world without end. Amen.

Intercession

We beseech you, most merciful God, for all peoples everywhere and for their health and for their hope and for their good. We desire with longing hearts that the blind see, the lame walk, and the dead arise in the blessed resurrection. We ask that troubled minds be restored, that hatreds between persons and nations be done away, that those shaken by fears learn again to trust you in all times and places. And finally we beseech you to help us all in the changing landscapes of body and soul to discern the ways that stand against confusion, the clearings in the chaos; through Jesus Christ our Lord. Amen.

* * *

Lord God, hear us as we pray for others—those in any distress of body, mind, or estate, those who are anxious for their lives, those who do not know where their daily bread will come from. Preserve in us, we pray, a sense of stewardship for that part of the world's wealth over which we have control. May we use it always for your purposes of love and justice. May no selfishness of our own make us callous toward those in need, no greed make us resent those whose poverty lays claim to our conscience and our goods. Amen.

Intercession

Sovereign Lord, enter with thy grace this time of our intercessions. Inform them with an abiding compassion for all this day who are in any need or trouble, those who are anxious, those who are in despair, so that in thy strength we may become instruments of thy healing, bearers of thy peace. Hear thou the cries of all the lost across the world and hold in mercy the peoples everywhere who are torn by warfare, pestilence, or fear. Even so, for us in our weakness, be thou a stay against our confusions and a true refuge against all our hours of desperation. Blessed is thy name. Amen.

* * *

Come, O Magnificence, to this occasion of our prayers. Hear us for the sake of all peoples everywhere—for the sick that they be healed, for the lonely that they be comforted, for the lost that they be found. Persuade in us every desire to build up rather than to tear down, every impulse to enfold rather than to break apart, every intention to be for rather than to be against. And as a church make us to be sanctuary, hospital, hope—a community to save, heal, and give promise; through Christ our Lord. Amen.

Intercession

Vast Lord, we beseech you for all the peoples everywhere and for all the needs, hidden and manifest, that afflict them and us—the aches and fevers of the body that they may be healed, the mind's terror that it shall be removed far from us, the heart's loneliness that it shall be comforted. As you are just, bring your righteousness against all within us that damages or disdains life, and your jubilance to all that upholds it. As you are merciful, persuade us to the ways of compassion for each other and for all persons far and near; through Christ our Lord. Amen.

* * *

Gracious Lord, we beseech thee for all peoples in all times and places, desiring to believe and hold in our hearts that every one counts in thy mercy. We pray for people we have never seen that their thirst be assuaged, their hunger fed, their wounds healed, and their very souls given cause for rejoicing. And we pray that we shall aways be compassionate as we look out upon the needs of humanity or look inwardly to our own needs. Pity us our frailties of body and spirit whoever we may be. Defend us from the evil, the terror, the darknesses that fear the light; and so we pray for everyone; through Christ our Lord. Amen.

Intercession

Dear God, let the sickness be healed, the death wish go from us, and the peoples come alive again. Let your word of hope sound in the cities and the voice of your mercy comfort the towns. Make us all teachable that we may learn again and again what things come first, what truths endure, what actions are worthy of your grace. Give us this day bread, joy, and vision; and so we pray for all; through Jesus Christ our Lord. Amen.

* * *

Tenderest Lord, we pray for all who are sick, deprived, or grieving (and especially for _____). The discomforted come to you, O God; the grieving seek your comfort; those deprived of their sustenance look to you for justice and restoration. Be all in all, we pray—a presence of love to those in pain, a strength to the bereaved, a vindication to the oppressed. By your loving justice fill our deepest needs, those we know and those we cannot name. And to us all bring the promise of the risen Lord that we will never be left without a Comforter. Amen.

Petition

Almighty God, who gathers us into thy church that by hymns we may praise thee and by prayers make known to thee our needs and our care for the several needs of peoples everywhere: bless us now with that grace which moves us from words to works. And whether we are silent or mumble, whether we are eloquent or groan, let there be in us always a mighty hope for the healing of all the lands, for the days when joy shall prosper, and for the hour when the nations shall know and practice peace. Amen.

* * *

Vast God, let it be yourself breaks through our prayers that what we cry out for the sake of the whole world carry a divine intention. Make us aware that as we know in ourselves the aches and torments of body and soul, so do all peoples everywhere. Stand us against the chicaneries of raw power, the limp falsehoods, the top secrets, the folly of little minds who pretend to lead. Give us that restlessness of being which always cares that the given joys of life flourish. And urge in us every strength to act out with and for others whatever we know and feel of thy presence among us; through Christ our Lord. Amen.

Petition

Come, brooding and majestic Lord, and inform the desperate mystery of our prayers. Set in our strengths your strength, in our loves your love, in our hopes your hope. Hear our cries for the sake of all peoples everywhere, for all those who have gone before us and for all those who will come after us. As you are the guardian of the universe, so keep this fragile earth from breaking and dispersing. Teach the nations and those who lead nations the things that make for peace, and help us to know the time of our visitation. Walk in our neighborhoods; through Christ our Lord. Amen.

* * *

O Lord, be with us so that we feel thee like hands upon us; uphold us so that we know thee like strength beneath us; go with us so that we have thee like love within us. Be for us in our goodness and against us in our evil. Keep us from all things shallow and unholy, and move our wills to seek the deep being of thyself. Protect us from all times and places that destroy and deceive, and give us grace to show the justice and mercy to all people that we would ask for ourselves. Make fruitful our prayers; through Jesus Christ our Lord. Amen.

Petition

Come to our prayers, great Lord, that in them we may speak boldly for the needs of one another and seek thy presence and thy strength for the mending and renewal of the bent world. Make of us a church whose very sighs, public and private, are for our own lives to heal, to gather in love, and bring hope. And keep us a people open to all the varied weathers that brood in human hearts and souls, that in us, by thy grace, the lost and the lonely and the fearful may find a solace and a clarity and a new beginning, even Jesus Christ our Lord. Amen.

* * *

O Lord, we pray for all those who are tossed about and helpless in the world—the victims of war and catastrophe, whose lives have been scored by the loss of loved ones; the pleasure seekers, who are the captives of their own appetites and the victims of desire; the mentally ill, whose anguish and fear are inescapable, whether waking or sleeping; the poor and impoverished, whose powers and labor are exploited by the rich. Help of the helpless, do thou abide with them, comforting them with thy love, and with thy wrath quickening the hearts of those who can change the conditions of life which bind them. Amen.

The Lord's Supper

Come, Holy Spirit, and make in us a holy preparation for this food of earth and heaven set before us. Let the loaf and the crusts bespeak both the feast and the famine. Let the cup running over wound us for the sake of those who thirst. Cause us to be nourished by such grace as was given before the foundations of the worlds that, as we are saviored, we may go forth to save; and give into our hands the drink of rejoicing whereby, with Christ, we overcome our death. Amen.

* * *

Almighty God, who calls us to this feast where mercy is enfleshed and love spilled endlessly: so let that mercy embody us that day by day we take into ourselves the world's sorrow, and so let that love burn within us that we spend ourselves to heal the world's brokenness. Give our prayers the spaciousness which includes all sorts and conditions of people, and urge in us every desire to do what our words beseech. Make known to us in this holy food the timeless meanings of thyself; through Jesus Christ our Lord. Amen.

Alas, great Lord, we are that people who have set our hearts after vain things and labored for the bread which does not satisfy. We have neglected the deep heavens thou hast placed in our own hearts, and we have neither proclaimed thy glory in the daylight nor meditated upon thy mercies in the night watches. We are hungry for life in the midst of plenty, and our souls are parched. Grant us, then, thy pardon that we may dare to take unto ourselves the bread and cup of thy salvation, that hereafter we shall hunger after righteousness and thirst only for thy grace; through Jesus Christ who invites us to this feast. Amen.

* * *

Almighty God, we confess that we are a fluttering people, both for and against you, both desiring and not desiring your merciful judgments, both hoping and despairing that you will invade us. We live haunted by the world's violence and the nations' pride, and we know, to our sorrow, our part in crippling others and breaking the peace. We ask for pardon for what we have done and left undone and will do again, and we beseech you that this feast of wound and forgiveness will become in us a healing of our sins, a deepening down, an opening out, even the way of Jesus Christ our risen Lord. Amen.

The Lord's Supper

Let us hold thanksgiving at Christ's feast, and give praise for bread that shows how heaven is bound to earth and for wine that reveals how earth is held in heaven. And let us heartily rejoice that here, in visible things, God comes among us that we shall be healed of those invisible sicknesses of soul and mind that have afflicted us. Especially let us be glad that in this hour we have a foretaste and promise of the timeless joy prepared for all peoples from the foundation of the world. Amen, amen, and amen.

* * *

Help us, great Lord, because the nations still rage in their folly, the people's eyes are blind, and the liberator has become the oppressor. Convert those who govern us from the wrong uses of power, the small and large tyrannies, the practice of the big lie. Cause us to feel in our bones the sorrows of the whole bent world, and persuade us to the healing. As you give us yourself in this bread of hope, this cup of mercy, so may we give ourselves to those who are without hope, to those who cry mercy; in the name of the Father, the Son, and the Holy Ghost. Amen.

Prayer Before the Sermon

O God, whose mercies are in, under, over, and beside all things and peoples: let thy Word move among the words spoken in thy name this day that they bear, though brokenly, the mark of thy truth, its fire, its vast intention. And persuade in the minds and hearts of all who hear a new desire to let thy truth break forth clamorously and with compassion in our homes, our neighborhoods, and our world. Amen.

* * *

God of all truth, let thy Word fall upon us like a rough and cleansing wind, dispersing our sins, scattering our vanities, uprooting our indifference that, shaken loose from our illusions, we shall be open to thy love and overtaken by thy truth, even Jesus Christ our Logos and our Lord. Amen.

* * *

Awaken us, O Lord of the universe, to hear in our hearts the true needs and longings that are there that, as thy holy Word is preached, we shall take its healing unto ourselves and go forth to live as people held in thy major promises, alive to all the promptings of heaven itself, and inwardly earnest to declare thee on the streets where we live. Amen.

Benediction

Go forth into the world in peace; be of good courage; hold fast to that which is good; render no one evil for evil; strengthen the fainthearted; support the weak; help the afflicted; honor all persons; love and serve the Lord, rejoicing in the power of the Holy Spirit; and the grace of the Lord Jesus Christ, the love of God, and the fellowship of the Holy Spirit be with you all. Amen.

* * *

God Almighty, bless us with the Holy Spirit; guard us in our going out and coming in; keep us ever steadfast in thy faith, free from sin and safe from danger; through Jesus Christ our Lord. Amen.

* * *

May the blessing of God Almighty, Father, Son, and Holy Spirit, rest upon us, and upon all our work and worship done in his name. May he give us light to guide us, courage to support us, and love to unite us, now and forevermore. Amen.

* * *

Now may the God of hope fill you with all joy and peace in believing, that you may abound in hope, and in the power of the Holy Spirit. Amen.

PRAYERS FOR
THE CHRISTIAN YEAR

Advent

Blessed is he who comes in the name of the Lord! Hosanna in the highest!

Once again, Lord God, we approach the birthday of your clarion Child, your Suffering Servant, your messenger Christ. Once again we make a place for him, however cluttered it may be with the pieces of our broken dreams, with unfinished resolves and fragments of love. Once again the bed we lay for him is as poor as any manger. But, Father of us all, we pray that he will come among us nonetheless, that his goodness will take hold in our hearts, his grace infect our wills, and his glory once more capture our imaginations.

Blessed is he who comes in the name of the Lord! Hosanna in the highest! Amen.

* * *

O Lord, the watchmen of ten thousand times ten thousand cities publish to the winter night the news of thy coming. Even so, we praise thee, Word of light to our darkness, Word of peace to our warfare, Word of love to our fear. Let carols sing, let prayers adore, let the whole earth rejoice and declare thee. Thou art fire and garland. Thou art the good Shepherd and the true King. With angels and archangels we adore thee, world without end. Amen.

Lord of the Advent, holy Invader, time's Comforter, O blessed Trinity: in thee all that ever was and is and shall be is made for shining. So do we praise thee for thy rage toward order before the universe was formed; so do we rejoice in the brightness of thy rising against all evil days; so do we praise thy coming in timelessness to capture time by love. In this dark century make us thy watchmen to proclaim thy light, set us as servants to prepare a table before thee, and in our human wilderness move us to clear a highway for our God. Amen.

* * *

Lord, thy season comes, thy fire, thy shout across our lonely night, and we are not ready. Alas, we are in a winter of fears; we are cold toward the stranger; we crowd toward emptiness. Caught up in the safe and mediocre, we avoid the vision; we miss the burning; we are deaf to the songs. We are ashamed. Now in this Advent we cry thy mercy and beseech thee that in us, once more, thy weather might browse and blow. Yea come, and grant us thy salvation; through Jesus Christ our Lord. Amen.

Advent

Lord, there is winter in us and grievous loneliness and dark that does not go away. Our souls ache, our understanding blurs, our sins increase; and in this season of thy coming we learn again how we have made a wasteland of the human heart and engaged in labors that do not satisfy. Come now, O Beloved, to our wilderness. Make in us the crooked paths straight and the rough places plain, and let your major voice that speaks comfort to our despair speak in us also the word of hope whereby we can enter our days with trust and the hours of our deaths with spacious expectation; through Jesus Christ our Lord. Amen.

* * *

Blessed Lord, in this season of thy coming the darkness in us deepens awaiting thy light, the evil in us trembles expecting thy mercy, the knowledge in us falters hearing thy truth. O we have sinned against innocence, forgotten human sorrow, denied pity, excused ourselves from love, and shunned holiness. Assail us by the bright blows of thy grace and make us teachable, that we may learn again the peace that comes on earth to people of goodwill; through Jesus Christ our Lord. Amen.

O Lord, in this alien time, this out-of-season century, this age absurd and wonderful and lost, we cry thy name whose name we cannot cry. O thou who art always coming, come! And give our voices praise and our eyes thy mystery. Let us taste thee in all our winter loneliness, and let us hear thee as a shout against our long despair—till touched by grace our griefs become our joys. Teach us to run with shepherds and to kneel with kings. Amen.

* * *

Come, Holy One, who hastens us now with cumbersome shepherds unto Bethlehem, come and abide in us that we learn again the things that make for our peace. Give us that listening which hears thy compassion moving through all human loneliness, and in the midst of the high music turn us towards the anguish of others. In the snowfall air, in the anxious dark, keep us open to neighbor and stranger, to angels and kings; and make us all ready for Christ's morning over Herod's earth. Amen.

Advent

Teach us, Lord God, how to wait faithfully and actively for the time of your coming. As we hear the celebrations sung through the ages, remind us that the tidings of great joy are being sung to our age as well, if we will but hear them and heed them. Prepare us to receive Christ when he comes to us as the innocent, as the jobless who has no place in our system, as the villager crucified by our weapons, as the stranger turned away from our friendship. Wherever he comes, in whatever guise, help us, Lord God, to know him, and knowing him to make a place for him in our hearts and in our lives. We pray in his own name and power. Amen.

* * *

Gracious Lord Jesus Christ, our host at every celebration of thy birth among us: do thou preside over our rites of joy during the holy days of Christmas. Purify our every desire; make all our giving an act of love and not a duty only; be present at our tables to teach us love for our loved ones; restrain us with the remembrance of those in the world whose need is as boundless as our abundance; and give us a holy joy in keeping this feast. So be our host and help us to celebrate thy coming in Bethlehem by being ready to receive thy coming in glory. Amen.

Christmas Eve Communion

Lord of the Christmas, whose largess enfolds us and whose mercies redeem us, we have dealt casually with thy coming among us and have turned each one to his own way. In the presence of spaciousness we have put on the small mind and shown the closed fist. Now in thee may our evil ways be scattered and our sins dispersed. Put far from us the lusts that harass us and the several greeds that control us. And gather us joyfully to thy high table where, in the food and drink of heaven, we shall know thy salvation for all peoples through the things of earth; through Jesus Christ, the Son of the Most High. Amen.

* * *

Lord, who in our wintertime sends Jesus to harry our countryside by grace and to refresh our tired cities as a fair wind: how can we but offer praises and glad hearts—for he shall dazzle us from the heights, yet settle close by us where we agonize and dream. So may we, in families and in neighborhoods across the world, find his mercy in our hearts and his jubilance, high and angel-tongued, a music in our flesh. Now in this bread and wine, broken and shared, let the major feast begin; and to thy name be honor and glory, dominion and power, forever and ever. Amen.

Christmas Eve Communion

Thou who gives us bread and drink and thereby heaven in our flesh and fire to burn away our dross: prepare us mightily to know together and with all the nations thy Comfort, timeless and unbegun, brimming and now. Urge in us every desire to enact thy word of love among those who are cast down, and send us forth to liberate the captives. Persuade us to the majesties of hope within us waiting to be born, and against the murk of indifference that surrounds us; let us with Christ be bearers of the light. Amen.

* * *

Praise to thee, thou far, thou near, for the mystery of thyself which begins, orders, and holds the utmost margins of space and time and all that lies therein, and for the gift of thyself that is resident among us, the Spirit that breathes into our being ancient strength and new possibilities! Praise, thou Incarnate, thou Son of man, for love made flesh and mercy walking and death undone! Praise, praise, praise, as the holy bread reaches us into timelessness and the eternal wine fires us to heal the sick and set the prisoners free! Amen.

Blessed Lord, who hath chosen earth as thy cradle and broken heaven in upon our drear captivity to sin and death: discover in us whatever grieves for the world's anguish, and deepen our sorrow for what we have done evilly to one another and for what we have neglected in the need of neighbor and stranger. Move us to a mighty repentance. Remove from within us the comfortable lies and the arrogance by which we have prevented the world's peace and damaged goodwill among the nations. Then set our hearts toward Bethlehem. Amen.

* * *

Ah, Jesukin, who in a rude barn gathers all creation: what shall we bring thee but sweet praise—for thou art the Word of heaven spoken across centuries; thou art the true Light who scans our darkness and scatters our despair; thou art the Savior who declares for the poor and brings hope to them that are cast down. At the Christmastide, in the astonished nights and the holy mornings, all that is shall praise thee. Yea, with archangels and great kings, with sparrows and shepherd folk, all tongues shall sing thee. Let the brimming world repeat the sounding joy. Glory to God in the highest! Amen.

Christmas Day

Lord, at thy parable of birth kneel us with all the families of earth in the presence of the Most High. Astonish us with the calms of heaven, and make of our hearts a resting and a listening place. Then, O gracious One, as thou hast imprinted in our flesh the glory of thy salvation, send us forth to make known thy wonderful works to the children of men. As we have been invaded by light, let us enlighten; as we have been found, let us seek out the lost; as we have been liberated, let us set the captives free. This we pray in the days of Christmas wherein all peoples have been given a garland of joy. Amen.

* * *

O God, what curious praise is ours for Jesus Christ— a red tricycle for small and busy feet, skis for a boy to ride the wind, some perfumes for the body's love, a large check for sweet charity, two hundred Christmas cards signed "love" by hand, letters to friends long lost in years ago, much weariness and ribbons and short tempers. O find in this, O find in this, dear Lord, our human hearts, our hope for all, our praise for thee. For we stumble in the busy ways and have a lonely carol to sing before the holy places; in Jesus' name. Amen.

O that our tongues were bells and our hands drums and our feet a dance and a leap that we might praise thee! Could the winter day but say for us our praise, or the brittle grass or the air on the blue jay's wing! Where is the music that shall sing thee? What word shall tell the heart's adoration? O Majesty, let us but kneel in the mind's dark, in the body's rush, in the soul's aloneness, and hear thee being born. Amen.

* * *

O God, whose birth startles us with glory that reaches heaven to earth, with hope that summons earth to heaven: we confess that we are ill at ease before thee, that we have resisted thy promises. We have been affluent but not amazed, learned but not wise, successful but not satisfied. O in this burning time break through our make-believe, confuse our arrogance, and where we are timid in faith strengthen us for a mighty praise. Persuade us to those high celebrations that desire for everyone a world at peace and thy salvation everywhere descending; through Jesus Christ our Lord. Amen.

Sundays after Christmas

O Lord God, in the presence of the Child, you have spoken to us with great tenderness, and we have answered with callousness. We confess that we have understood and still refused your call to deal tenderly with one another, to be peacemakers in the earth, to let justice roll down as waters and slake the thirst for righteousness in your world. Forgive us, we pray, and let a new birth of love happen in our lives now, as once it happened in that village stall. We pray in the name of the Child who is your Christ and our Lord, Jesus. Amen.

* * *

O promising God, whose message is our mandate—peace on earth: we confess that we have welcomed the words but resisted their cost, that we have declared for peace but justified our wars. Once again in this season of remembrance and hope make our festivities recall that it was for peace that he came, for peace that he died, and for peace that he now both lives and suffers. May the justifications of violence go dry in the mouths of those who speak them; the peddlers of arms find no market for their goods; the old hatreds make sense no longer; the new hopes be irrepressible. Then we will sing, Hosanna! Blessed is he who comes in the name of the Lord! Hosanna in the highest! Amen.

Lord God, who came among us in a simple circumstance, then in a cowshed, now in a tenement room or a mud hut; who had the freedom to be poor, to be faithful, to die with integrity: be with us now to open our hearts to thy promise that, where we love one another in thy name, there wilt thou be in the midst of us. Grant us open ears, open minds, and open hearts, that the music of thy praise will echo the praises of our lives. Grant this, O Father, in the name of Jesus, whom we honor as thy Son and claim as our Lord. Amen.

* * *

O Almighty God, who by the birth of the holy Child Jesus has given us a great light to dawn on our darkness: grant, we beseech thee, that we may walk in his light to the end of our days. Bestow upon us, we beseech thee, that most excellent gift of charity to all people, that the likeness of thy Son may be formed in us and that we may have the ever-brightening hope of eternal life; through Jesus Christ our Lord. Amen.

Sundays after Christmas

Heavenly Father, again we hear the ancient promise of peace on earth sung against the noise of war, and of goodwill toward men said against the record of our inhumanity. May thy gracious promise and thy tender love once more set hope alive in us; and having heard thy Son's birth announced in this clamorous world, may we be encouraged to believe in thy love, to have faith in thy promises, to build in our hearts and in our neighborhoods a safe manger in which to lay our newborn hope for a world where thy glory will shine round about. Amen.

* * *

O God our Father, who has visited and redeemed your people, and has called on us to be redemptive forces in your world: help us, we pray, that the visions and hopes of this season will not fade after the twelfth day, nor the plodding, indulgent, and cruel realities take over again, unchallenged by the angels' song and the child's faith. By the power of your presence, Lord God, may the ceremonies of the season be more than ceremonies. May they call up in us new determination to live by our vision and persevere by our faith. Amen.

Epiphany

O God, we praise thee for thyself in whom we live and by whom all things are sanctified and made for shining. We praise thee for this day which proceeds from thy bounty and returns to thy love. We praise thee for every moment when the work of our hands is blessed beyond our deserving and for every hour that our hearts are made glad by a wise and endless peace we did not earn. Amen.

* * *

O Comforter, who from the other side of dark invades our despair, our loss, and who overcomes for all the harried people the disasters of nations, the defeats of flesh and soul: now in the brimming days that hasten us towards Bethlehem all life shall praise thee—the star-lost skies, the turning earth abounding in all weathers, twelve-winded airs across the valleys blowing, and everywhere the new dance teaching marrow, bone, and once again the new rejoicing firing our hearts; through Jesus Christ our Lord. Amen.

Epiphany

Now, Lord, hear our confession and receive our sorrow for our dullness, our stupidity, our fraud. Yea, seeing you, all love, our sin is a heaviness upon us and in us. We are a very winter of gray and cold. We live half-seeing, half-hearing, half-knowing, half-believing. Pity us. Awaken us. Save us. Be archangel in us till we dare to soar, and in all the plodding times and places of the months ahead be to us unicorn and dove and storm and star until our flesh becomes your wild, wise Word. Amen.

* * *

Glory be to thee, O Lord our God, whose face is ever hidden from us, but whose will and love have been made known to mighty kings and simple shepherds. We come before thee not as wise but as seeking. Grant us the wisdom to glory only in thee—in thy judgment which condemns our foolishness and in thy love which comforts our suffering—that having learned to adore thee, we may find that our seeking ends in praise of thee who has long sought us in Jesus Christ our Lord. Amen.

Epiphany

O Lord our God, who by the light of a star has dispelled the night of our fears and made us free to sing again: we give thanks that once more the weight of glory is pressed upon an inglorious world, that a stirring is in our midst and a hope is rising to strive against the world's despair. Be active in our minds and hearts, Lord God, so that no distress will prevent us from doing the works of light and of life, no impatience keep us from the slow work of building a place where love will be the mandate we obey. Amen.

* * *

Lord God, who promised that your glory should be revealed and that all flesh should see it together: set a restlessness stirring in our hearts, a waiting for the light that will break into our darkness, a wondering before the innocence that will address our sinful world, a waking to the hope that will dispel our weariness in seeking your kingdom above all things. Glory to God in the highest! Amen.

Ash Wednesday

Almighty God, as we enter the days of penitence our fault is upon us, for we know well the desert places, the wild beasts, the satanic murmurings. We are afraid in the silences. We have refused others our hearts. We have fawned over the demons that promise power. We feel the wrath. Gracious Lord, create in us now a great repentance wherewith we can stand against the evil one, move with love through the terror and the drab hours, and trust in your promises—resonant and redemptive among all things and people, world without end. Amen.

* * *

Our sins are upon us, O Lord; their dark hovers over us, and their evil prowls in us. We confess them, that they turn us from thee, and so from what is holy and pure; we acknowledge them, that they divide us from others, and so from pity and compassion; we fear them, that they carry in them a torment; we repent them, that they bear against us a judgment. O gracious One, recover us from the principalities and powers, this death in life, this chaos that destroys us, and grant us thy forgiveness which cleanses and thy pardon which sets us free, even Jesus Christ our Lord. Amen.

Praise be to thee, O Lord our God, who art the rest of the weary, the refreshment of those for whom the world has grown old too early. Praise be to thee, thou Judge of all, who hast given us thy law to guide our lives and thy love to support us in walking according to thy law. Praise be to thee, O God our Redeemer, who daily calls us into a new path of life, lived by courage and faith in thy never-ending love. Amen.

* * *

O Lord our God, whose Son Jesus Christ has gone before us into the desert of temptation, who has ascended one hill to be transfigured and another to be crucified: we praise thee without ceasing that thou hast been our God and our Savior, that thou didst give us one man with truly clean hands and a pure heart, one like us in human needs and freedom, yet without guile. For him who lived and died for us, and liveth for us evermore, we praise thee now and always. Amen.

Lent

O God, who by the example of thy Son, our Savior Jesus Christ, teaches us the greatness of true humility, and calls us to watch with him in his passion: prepare us by faith in him to meet the crises of our own lives with steadfast endurance, even as he has showed us. We confess that we have not been faithful under trial, that we blow hot or cold as seems expedient, and that under the least adversity we quickly abandon whatever measure of self-forgetfulness we have achieved. O Lord, forgive us who cannot watch one hour, who have not been faithful to thee in thy trial when we could not stand fast in our own. And may thy forgiveness, ever-renewed, be our occasion for repentance and rededication. Amen.

* * *

O most merciful Lord, who through thy Son faced temptations in the wilderness, and who knows the temptations that beset us daily: grant us grace to stand so surely in our faith that we may bring to every temptation both courage of spirit and strength of will, never surrendering to those desires which violate thy love for us. May the knowledge and example of Christ so fill us that we will set ourselves gladly to the tasks of prayer and meditation and self-discipline by which we are strengthened during these days of Lent. Amen.

Almighty God, we give you thanks that Jesus called you Father and taught us to address you with the intimacy of daughters and sons. We are grateful for the images of your love and acceptance he conveyed by his stories, and for the knowledge that we are invited to take up his way of self-understanding and self-acceptance. Enable us to see the call to repentance as an invitation of the waiting Father, and teach us to use the days of Lent to ready our response. Amen.

* * *

O God our Father, whose Son trod the path to death and met eternal life, who passed through the darkness of crucifixion to live in the light of resurrection, and who taught us to choose the hard road of self-examination and repentance that leads to true knowledge of ourselves and forgiveness: grant us this day and all the days of Lent the wisdom to see our need for repentance, the strength to renounce those things which we know to be evil, and the grace to seek thy forgiveness for the evil we do unwittingly. So by the path that leads through the trial of our spirits do thou grant us the gift of thy Holy Spirit which is eternal life. Amen.

Palm Sunday

God of the deep heavens, who places the eternal where
people work and children play: praise for this day of
waving palms, small beasts, and hopeful voices; praise
for the divine foolishness upsetting our poise; praise
for the divine patience that teaches us to endure;
praise for colors, distance, somersaults, sing-song,
dance; praise for all that is capering and playful
whereby the confined are set free and the solemn
vanishes away! Hosanna! Glory to God in the highest!
Amen.

* * *

Lord of the quiet way, we confess the sins, deliberate
and vain, by which we have diminished others and
made ourselves most miserable. And we are aware to
our shame how our heavy-handedness has destroyed
gentleness and despoiled the holy. Alas, in these
feverish times, our stupidity has allowed us to pay
court to demagogues and to count too much on the
arithmetics of power. We have progressed to fear. We
have achieved thin souls. May the High King of heaven
forgive us; may he tutor us in humility; may he marry
us to the divine love, even Jesus Christ our Lord.
Amen.

Lord God, whose Son we hailed and crucified: we confess our inconstancy in faith. We have been loud with convictions and weak in performance of the works of love. We have been quick in saying and sluggish in doing what is right. We have nothing wherewith to lay claim on thy love. Forgive us, we beseech thee, as thou didst forgive the multitude that strewed thy path first with palms and then with derision. And as thou didst raise up thy Son, first on a cross and then on thy right hand, raise us up, we pray, from the sin into which we have fallen. Restore us to thyself and thus to new life, that we may be bold to live by thy grace. Amen.

* * *

O God our Sovereign, we give thanks for this day of triumph and tragedy, when glory and sorrow are mixed, when courage and fear are met together. We are grateful, O Lord, for that humble procession we recall, for it is a symbol to us of your own costly and redeeming presence in this world of wheat and tares. Now help us, good Lord, in our minds and hearts to understand that just as you have entered the city of hope and of trial so we are called to take up our work in an imperfect world, not waiting for the kingdom of righteousness but working for it, not turning away from hard demands but accepting them in confidence that you are with us unceasingly. Amen.

Palm Sunday

O God, who has brought us to this holy time wherein we renew the memory of our Redeemer's passion: enable us, we pray, to enter fully the drama of redemption in the coming days. Make vivid to us the suffering to which thy Son was put on our account and on our behalf, and vivid too the victory of life over death which he vouchsafed to us once and for all when he abandoned his tomb for a throne. By this may our faith be brightened and our obedience strengthened. All this we ask in the name of Jesus Christ. Amen.

* * *

O God, come to us this day in the parable of the meek King. Lift up our eyes always to the green tree. Give us the patience for burden and sadness of the small beast. Quicken us to the hidden laughter. Surprise us by joy. And against our walled cities, our regiments of fear, our committees of pride let the children come, and the dances of trust, and the somersaults of hope. Let the meek King be heard. Amen.

Maundy Thursday

Blessed be thou, O God of the universe, who sets the seed of the wheat and grape in the ground to die that they may bring forth and nourish life. Blessed be thou, O God of our salvation, who in this Eucharist feeds us the bread and wine of earth that in them we may know the meat and drink of heaven and be strengthened. Blessed be thou, O God of our liberation, who sanctifies these elements by the divine love that suffers with all sufferers and by the divine truth that sets all peoples free. Amen and amen and amen.

* * *

How marvelous thy mercy, O Lord, that from our separate, casual, and crooked ways calls us to thy table, thy high feast of grace, thy plain meal of forgiveness. And here we are as Peter who denied thee thrice; as John and James, priding to be first; as Matthew, publican and sinner; as Judas with his kiss of death; as everyman tangled in self-love, self-pity, and dark fear. O by thy bread put flesh on the ribs of our thin souls, and from thy cup pour fire to kindle us to be thy people, eager for joy and faithful in adoration. Amen.

Maundy Thursday

O God, our God, blessed, all-wise, and eternal: hear our confession, and by such mercies as we cannot give one another save us from our sins; for we persist in our darknesses and tangibly break and destroy the flesh of the world and the souls of its people. We continue the wars; we live off the misery of others; we permit the comfortable lies. Even more, we wear the masks of righteousness and absolve ourselves from the crimes. Now as we eat and drink the broken bread and the wine of suffering, so nourish us that we desire again to risk ourselves for healing, even as Jesus who on the dark tree broke himself for all the earth. Amen.

* * *

O God, we come to thy mighty table with sin in us and around us. We carry havoc in the blood which is against thee. We dwell among people who forget thee. We are indifferent and have no peace. We burn but bear no light. We feel the utter desolation. Yet we are bound to thee as by a mystery, thou who art our peace, the light that shineth in the dark. Feed us thy daylight in this bread, the fire of heaven in this cup, even Jesus Christ who is the world's consolation. Amen.

Hear, mighty Lord, how with one voice we speak our sorrow for our sins, those darknesses within that we set between ourselves and thee. O we are creatures of the little prides, the lazy mind, the meager trust, and the envious heart. The muddled world that we fear is our own creation. We are matted in by stupidities and nighted in by blindness. Take us now, thou majestic and merciful One, and teach us the hard lesson of forgiveness. Let the love we deny save us, even Jesus Christ our Lord. Amen.

* * *

Lord God, whose messenger among us was a man of sorrows and one acquainted with grief, by whose stripes we are healed: hear us on this Day of Sorrows as we pray for all who bear the burdens of grief through the loss of loved ones or through bitter disappointment. Help them, O God, first by the knowledge that they do not carry their burdens alone, and then by the love that others bear them at the time of their trials. May all who sorrow know again that nothing in all creation can separate us from your love, which is in Christ Jesus our Lord. Amen.

Easter

Incarnate One, thou Servant broken on the tree, thou
God assaulting death for all our sakes: triumphals,
trumpets declare thee; bells, clamorous songs, all
breath and tongues across the earth, the earth itself
and all that is therein praise thy holy resurrection.
Receive from us now, most blessed Lord, a jubilance
above all other joys; for by thine Easter thou hast
awakened all peoples to immortality, released our
hearts from fear, and taught us the ways of thy
compassion. Therefore, we give thee thanks and endless adoration that all flesh shall at the last days stand,
forgiven and loved, in the presence of the risen Lord,
unto whom with thee and the Holy Ghost be all glory
and honor, dominion and power, forever and ever.
Amen.

* * *

Praise be to thee, O sovereign and majestic Lord; for in
our rising thou art our strength, and in our going about
thou art our protector, and in our falling thou art our
deliverer. Though the air split with fire and the
mountains of death arise around us, thou wilt dispel
misery, thou wilt take away fear, and thou wilt con-
quer death. Praise be to thee! Amen.

Vast God, receiver of our sins and sorrows, assailant and conqueror of our deaths: now at your Easter we are ashamed of all within and about us that is shallow and corrupt and without hope. We have avoided you, and therefore have absented us from depth and the abiding. We have coveted our own well-being and too zealously blamed the time's illnesses on others. We have yielded to cynicism and fear. Now among the alleluias, we repent us many things and seek again that forgiveness which kills all death and sets the prisoners free, even Jesus Christ our pardon and our peace. Amen.

* * *

O God, how can we come before thee in sin who so rarely approach thee in adoration? O the wrong in us is great! We have been busy with the art of self-pity, the enjoyment of our angers, the feeding of our prejudices. We have wasted our days and dreaded our nights. We feel baffled, troubled at heart, and useless. Turn us now from the tangle and the idolatry to a plain path, to a trust in thee, and transform us by the steady arm of thy forgiveness into new men and women validly alive in all times and places because we are alive in thee; through Jesus Christ our resurrected Lord. Amen.

Easter

We give thanks, O Lord of the universe, that now and at the hour of our death you have provided the mighty resurrection for us and for all peoples, whereby according to your compassion the dead shall break forth into new life, and death shall have no dominion. We give thanks for the immortality always within us whereby we transform the world and its accidents and handle time and its stress and strain. Christ being raised from the dead, we give thanks that we are called as by trumpets and divine laughter to trust the days, honor the seasons, and believe in the coming age. Alleluia! Amen.

* * *

Gracious heavenly Father, who creates new life in us daily and promises that new life with thee is our final destiny: we pray thee for all who are bereaved (and especially for _____). Heed their sorrows. Grant unto them, and to all who look into the bleak mystery of death, to see behind its dark visage the light of thy redeeming promise. Renew their hearts with a sure confidence that as all the world rests in thy providence so their loved ones rest now in thy loving presence. May the rejoicing of this day lift them from their sorrow into a new light of life. Amen.

Almighty God, the Lord and Giver of Life, in the joy of this Easter morn may we see ourselves anew in the mirror of the resurrection. Help us to open our reluctant spirits to the glad tidings of this day, that they may be sustained with the sacrament of gratitude and praise. Strengthen us to live a holy life now. May we learn again to walk with eager steps, as those who have been healed, who have heard the shouts of victory, who look to the day when every worldly care dissolves and every selfish concern is crowded out by thy presence. All this we pray in the name of him who is Victor over death, and Lord over life. Amen.

* * *

Gracious Lord, who intends that every hour wear the eternity of Easter: enter our prayers so that we speak as people of the resurrection who expect and hope for what they ask. Yet keep our concerns worthy of the calling to which we are called, and make our flesh and our wills ready to act on our words. As we beseech you for all in the world that needs mending, and for strength and hope to do our part and more, we ask especially that the world be rebuked, chastened, and loved into discovering again its true purpose in the praise of God and the love of persons; through Jesus Christ our risen and redemptive Lord. Amen.

Pentecost

Almighty God, who gathers us into thy church that by
hymns we may praise thee and by prayers make known
our needs and the several needs of peoples everywhere:
bless us now with that grace which moves us from
words to works. And whether we are silent or mumble,
whether we are eloquent or groan, let there be in us
always a mighty hope for the healing of all the lands,
for the days when joy shall prosper, and for the hour
when the nations shall know and practice peace.
Amen.

* * *

Lord God of justice and of peace, we ask once more for
thy tongues of fire to preserve us from the fire of our
own tongues. Consume our hatreds lest they consume
us, and by the power of thy presence check all un-
bridled expression of our own power. Give us patience,
wisdom, and hearts so enflamed by thy grace that we
will speak with restraint and listen with compassion.
Breathe thy Whitsun Spirit into our common lives
both now and always. Amen.

Lord God, who hast called us to be one in thy church, and thy church to be one with the sufferings and needs of the world: grant us grace to see thee by seeking opportunity to do thy will. May thy people be known by their readiness to bear one another's burdens, to seek and serve the cause of justice, and to witness well their concern for peace. Amen.

* * *

Come, Holy Spirit, and help us to desire with a complete desire the health and happiness of all peoples. Cause us to care mightily that wars cease, that injustice fail, that the fear which troubles our hearts goes from us. Teach us by sign and gesture, word and silence, to know in our flesh the anguish that is in the world, to make it ours, and as a church to act in ways that heal, give hope, and renew; through Jesus Christ our Lord. Amen.

Pentecost

Lord God, who came to a scattered people and made them one with each other in understanding and in love, and who with tongues of fire fell upon men and women and consumed the walls of confusion which divided them from each other and isolated them from thy love: receive our thanks that thou hast been among us and that we can now take hope. We pray for the renewal of thy presence as a fire to consume the walls of hatred, fear, falseness, and arrogance by which people are scattered, becoming enemies to each other and to themselves. Lord God, by thy power divisions were overcome but each one's dignity and honor were preserved. Be it so again, we pray. Let that great unity prevail in thy church, and by its witness in the world may such a unity prevail among all races and nations. We pray in the name and in the confidence of Jesus Christ our Lord. Amen.

* * *

O God the Creator, who hast made of one blood all the nations of the earth, and hast bound us together in the divine family as thy children: we pray for all who are alienated from their sisters and brothers, for all whose lives are discolored by hate or insistent pride, for the oppressor and the oppressed, the proud and the humiliated, the strong and the weak. Especially we pray that the wound of racial prejudice be healed wherever it is opened. And where prejudice spills over into conflict, chasten the powerful and strengthen the powerless, and give to both an honest desire for reconciliation without revenge. Amen.

Surely, O Magnificence, thy jubilate is sounding among us, thy music summons our days, and everywhere the mornings shout for joy. So may praise in us continue—in our handiwork as it serves thee, in our dreaming as it pleases thee, in our anguish as it trusts thee, in our loving as it honors thee. And so may our lives be visible thanksgivings for thyself who undergirds and saves. Amen.

* * *

O Lord God, in whom the whole world abides and who cares for its good: we adore thee who art our life's source, support, and end. When thou, our great Original, dost touch us through creation's beauty, we praise thee that we have our source in thee. When thou, O Holy Spirit, doth daily bless us with health, comfort, and a good hope, we praise thee that we have thy gracious promise of a Comforter to support us in our life. When thou, O Redeemer strong to save, doth refresh us with forgiveness and a new vision, we praise thee that our end is hid in thee. All laud and glory be to thee, thou one and blessed Trinity, in our time and in all ages. Amen.

Trinity Season

O thou Creator of all that is, we give thee thanks for the multitude of thy ways in coming to us. Grant us always such a clear eye and a single desire that we shall know thee and thy message of love and grace and help, in whatever language it is spoken, behind whatever appearance it takes. O thou who art one and holy, the Father, Son, and Holy Spirit, hear us, Triune God, and receive our praise; through Jesus Christ our Lord. Amen.

* * *

We thank you, Lord of the universe, keeper of the high spaces, watcher beyond time, for returning us from our summer journeys and bringing us once more to the windowed church, the family of friends, this place of our rejoicing. We praise you for this season that now waits upon the blazon trees, the fire tastes, the dark birds going down the ancient sky. We thank you and praise you for the great works before us, the new beginnings, hope riding on the mornings, and peace gathering us in the nightfalls of a million stars. Amen.

Almighty God, whom angels sing and peoples everywhere acclaim: we pray unto thy majesty and thy grace for this earth beset by earthquakes and famine, the nations broken by war, the peoples crippled by disease and fear. Protect us when Nature goes berserk, and spare the innocent. Teach all lands a sweet reasonableness and a desire to live as one world under thy generous laws. Return the sick to health, and renew in all of us the spirit of hope, the desire for comradeship, the power of rejoicing. Amen.

* * *

Praise now the Creator, who before all time spoke the beginning, voiced the stars into place, and gathered on earth adroit beasts, singing birds, dolphins and terrapins, the trees shaking out shade or catching winter snows. Praise the Lord who springs in us the body's fire, the heart's dream, and the soul's adventure. Praise him who laughs at the nations, who watches the cities rise and diminish, who takes the villages into his arms. Praise the majestic One who, among darkness and power, turns our history again towards himself that all the peoples shall be saved. Amen. Amen. Amen.

All Saints

O Lord our God, we rejoice in the communion of all thy saints, of prophets and apostles, of martyrs steadfast under trial and ordinary men and women who were found. Enable us, we pray, to draw inspiration and courage from them, and in our own lives to praise thee for the eternal joy that is both theirs and ours. Amen.

* * *

Bind us together, Lord God, with all who have come before us, whose rest is now in your presence, and with all who live out their hopes and trials in other lands and places, whose names we do not know, whose faces we have not seen, but with whom we are all one people, all your children. May we have communion with them in our thoughts and prayers, and share the bread of life with them to the praise of your glory. Amen.

PRAYERS FOR SPECIAL
OCCASIONS

New Year's Day

O God, our days go by as a dream and the seasons run swiftly on and are gone, and we do not turn to thee nor hear thy Word nor look for thee in the night watches. We walk in the mazes of our own vanity. We listen to the prattle of foolish men. And in the dark of our own dark, we look into our own blind eyes. O holy, high, and mighty Lord, break us loose from our folly. Capture us by grace and hold us in mercy, lest our years go by empty, drab, and lost. Save us through Jesus Christ our Lord. Amen.

* * *

Like Abram's journey, the year before us brims with promise and uncertainty. So, Lord God, we pray for a good passage through it, drawn by new questions and safe from absurd conclusions. Help us daily to measure our pursuits by our best commitments, and finally to learn from one another how to journey in the world as those who love it well and serve it wisely. Amen.

God of power and glory, who led your children out of bondage with a cloud by day and a pillar of fire by night: lead us, we pray, out of bondage to the mean goals and small-minded desires which propel nations into war. Make us be servants of peace, reluctant to force our wills on others, quick to honor the hopes and integrity of our neighbor nations in this small world, and always more ready to build than to destroy. Grant us grace to be proud but not arrogant, loyal but not blind, dutiful but not slavish, so that we may honor our flag by giving it second place to your peaceable design for the world. Amen.

* * *

Almighty God, who governs the nations with justice and mercy: accept our thanksgiving for this land in all its promise, chaos, failure, and fulfillment, and hold in your foreverness the sweep, height, and hope that is America. Help us to honor those who have broken and cleared the way before us—voyagers and exiles, school-teachers and minutemen, liberators who fashioned just laws. Deepen in us the excitement of clipper ships and Moby Dick, wagons west and cattle drives, Walden and the sprawling railroads. Make us penitent in remembrance of those robbed and plundered, massacred and driven, harried and enslaved—victims who paid the price of others' greed. Still keep our hearts glad and grateful for the dead and the living who gave and continue to give their talent, service, and life itself to the dream of this nation as sanctuary for the oppressed and homeland for the free. Amen.

Commencement

Lord God, we pray for wisdom, now that our learning is well begun. We pray for insight, now that we have learned to be attentive. And now that we know something of justice, art, nature, society, and the human heart, we pray for a lifelong commitment to make good use of what we understand. Through what we value, may true values be seen. Through what we do with our lives, may walls of misunderstanding be breached, old prejudices destroyed, and new visions emerge of a world where charity takes preeminence over power and righteousness will be both politic and possible. We pray for thy name's sake, for our own sake, and for the sake of our inheritance. Amen.

* * *

Come now, vast God, to this high occasion, to this university (college, school) that celebrates its virtues, praises its scholars, anoints its students, and crowns its honored guests. May the university (college, school) be always spokesman for the Good, the True, and the Beautiful. Around the footnotes let some flesh and humanity cling, and in the laboratories raise the question of purpose. Set loose in the classroom the wild airs of open discussion, variety, dissent, ideas old and new. Keep learning and life comrade and close. Make compassion more important than sophistication and the delighted heart more significant than a passing grade. Finally, as this day exclaims itself, defend us from the clichés and gather us in love. Amen.

Vast God, as with each breath we have need of thee, remind us that we have a need of one another; that we have need of a great vision whereby this marvelous, chaotic, dreaming America comes true in our flesh; that we have a need to forgive one another because we are human beings, not gods; that we have a need to honor all persons. Therefore, daily and hourly brood among the various peoples of this land, continuing us always in that unity of life that arises out of patience with one another's differences and out of concern to enact generously whatever advances the common good. And unto thee be all the praise. Amen.

* * *

Defend, O Lord, this gracious land from misuse of power, distrust of neighbor and stranger, corruption of the marketplace, the illusions of wealth; and give unto those allowed to govern us a due respect for thy sovereign rule over all nations, including our own, that they may be guided always by thy compassion for all peoples, thy vision of peaceable towns and cities everywhere, thy claim upon us to be a servant nation for the sake of all the world. Then by thy strength enable us to enact in our lives a patriotism whose first allegiance is to thy laws and thy ways; through Jesus Christ our Lord. Amen.

Independence Day

Lord God, before whose everlasting glory the nations rise and pass away: we pray for the grace to know and the will to do the things of honor, equity, and compassion while our nation lives. As our founders worked to form a nation, let us work to form a family of nations. As they hoped for a place where free souls could live in dignity, let us be animated by the same hope and erase the indignities still inflicted on poor and outcast peoples. As they brought great courage and imagination to their tasks, help us to bring the same to ours, lest by small minds and selfish prudence we waste our inheritance. Amen.

Labor Day

God of the continents, whose mighty acts continue to astound us: enter the celebrations of this Labor Day to bless those men and women who, across this goodly land, work faithfully to provide bread for the nation and those things needful for the well-being of all the world. Help us who receive so much at their hands to honor them and to support them by every honest means toward safe working conditions, fair wages, and satisfactions in the labor undertaken and accomplished. And command us to march hand in hand toward this nation's declared purposes of liberty and justice for all. Amen.

Opening of a School Year

Lord God, in a world where justice has not yet rolled down as waters nor righteousness as a mighty stream, where knowledge floods in but there is only a trickle of wisdom, we pray for this school, its students and teachers and administrators, and for the task in which we now join. Turn our efforts to good, so that as our understanding increases, our sense of responsibility will deepen, and we will finish the coming year having made the world more habitable and ourselves more humane. We pray this, O God, for our own sakes, and for the sake of the future you have given us to create. Amen.

United Nations Day

O Lord our God, who dost most marvelously work out the reconciliation of all peoples through thy living word: bring thy word to bear with power, we pray, on the United Nations and on all those who sit in its councils. Instill in them such awe of thy power that they will use their own power responsibly to advance justice and establish peace in the relations among nations. We beseech thee to hear our prayer, as we also thank thee that thou hast assured us that our prayers are heard through the perfect mediation of Jesus Christ our Lord. Amen.

Election Day

Lord God, by whose providence all things are ordered, in whose love all things find their purpose, under whose justice all our purposes are judged: we pray for our nation at a time of decision. May each of us recall that the power of our vote is not a political opportunity but a sacred obligation. Help us to examine both issues and persons with a fresh and open mind, not being captive either to our own past commitments or to narrow self-interest. May the great hopes of our faith motivate our choices, so that the cause of peace, of righteousness, and of justice for all your children will be strengthened by what we do. We pray in the name of Jesus Christ, in whom we are called to be both free and responsible. Amen.

Thanksgiving Day

Yea, thou Lord of us all; thou Sovereign of the air's ocean, the valley's running, the cumbersome mountains; thou Goodness in the taste of our souls: we praise thee for the clamorous and holy seasons; for the furrow, the stalk, the leaf, and the grain; and for the feast all gold and red and high. We praise thee for great mercy toward our sins, for constant love when we are in despair, for strength to rise again in the dark hour. We praise thee for thy peace against our wars, and for thy ways of peace that shall redeem nations. Amen.

Thou Lord of all that is, thou Creator of the air's ocean, thou Juggler of stars, thou whose voice murmurs its music throughout all the earth, thou high and holy One in whom we dream: surely and with exultations we name thy name with thanksgiving, we call out to thee with praise. We give thee thanks that thou hast set the fires of the blood, taught the mind to run, breathed in us souls. And we praise thee for families whereby we learn to love, and for neighborhoods wherein we learn to trust. Surely thy goodness and mercy is ever upon us, full measure, pressed down, and running over. Surely thy bounty is upon the land, thy sceneries within our hearts, thy compassion open across the whole bent world. Amen and amen and amen.

* * *

O God, our Source and our Hope, we give thanks for the ordinary and the extraordinary things that sustain us and make our lives rich and whole—for daily bread, and for the experience of discovering that it is a blessing; for friendships and duties, for good hopes and precious memories, for the gifts we give each other by our understanding of one another's hopes and hurts, for the rich variety of our experience as human beings, for the family reunions that mark this season. Help us by the power of your Spirit to act from gratitude, as befits those who have received the great gift of your Son, Jesus Christ. Amen.

Thanksgiving Day

Almighty God, we praise your name and glorify you, remembering your promise that while the earth remains, seedtime and harvest shall not fail. We bless you for the supports of this life, for the kindly fruits of the earth, for the food we too often receive without thanks and eat without remembering you. May gratitude be restored in us, we pray, and all our uses of this world's bounty be touched with thanksgiving. Then we will know that what we have is not our own alone, but ours to share as it is ours to use. Amen.

Closing of the Year

O timeless Lord of all our days and years, now as the twelvemonth closes and we remember and reflect, provide us with thyself as companion as we enter the new year. Put from us, in the mercy of thy means, the waste of hours, the dry seasons, the desolate evenings, and the shabby dawns. Go with us into the mystery of the days that run in haste before us. Show us the everlasting in the perishable, the hope in the defeat, the purpose in the chaos. Help us arise to each morning, glad that its seconds have the height of thine eternity; through Jesus Christ our Lord. Amen.

Baptism

As by thy mystery, most gracious Lord, thou hast used this brimming water to bring to this child the promises of heaven and revealed again the freshness of Eden among the things of earth, so we pray thee to encourage him (her) day by day and year by year toward thy goodness. Keep round about him (her) thy holy love that he (she) may enter life lovingly; teach him (her) thy mercy that he (she) may handle life mercifully; engage him (her) by thy truth that he (she) may grasp life truthfully. In all ways be to him (her) guide and protector that he (she) may awaken to daylights of hope and go to sleep in the sure faith that the universe itself rests on thy compassion; in the name of Jesus who blessed and delighted in all children. Amen.

Confirmation

We beseech thee, most bountiful God, to be in our prayers this day that, in its spirit of quiet jubilation over thy gift of these young people, we may pray aright for thy love, strengthening and sustaining them all the days of their lives. And we ask that they shall know the time of their visitation; that increasingly they shall learn the things which make for peace; and that, like Jesus, they shall embody in their flesh and hearts patience before their suffering, sure delight in each day's revelations, and abiding faith in thy presence always among us to heal and to renew. Keep them and us aware of the victories that come with trust; through Christ our Lord. Amen.

Marriage

God, who declared for holy love when Eden sang: anoint with generous blessing this man and this woman who, by a spacious trust in thee and one another, risk themselves together in the freedoms of marriage. Gather them to the lovely seasons of the flesh, to the awakenings to each other's dreams, to an awe before all mysteries given and received. Sing in their home the music of hospitality and true peace, and let them bring their shared affections to all life around them. Give them a patience in their time of stress and a gentleness toward the angers that would destroy them. And so deepen them in faith toward thee that theirs shall always be a household filled with praise; through Jesus Christ our Lord. Amen.

* * *

Lord God, we give thanks for the promise of this moment and we pray for _____ and _____ that they may be strengthened always to keep the covenant which they have made. May they be a blessing and a comfort to each other, the sharers of each other's joys, consolers to each other in sorrow, helpers to each other in all the chance and change of this life. May they encourage each other in their highest goals. May they trust each other and, trusting you as well, address their life with courage. May they not only accept but give affection to one another, and together have affection and consideration for those who come under their roof and into their circle. We join in prayer with those who are absent from us but present in spirit, and ask that the inspiration of this hour be not forgotten; through Jesus Christ our Lord. Amen.

On Establishing a Home

To live with thee, O Lord, is to be at home with ourselves. Now be with us, we pray, as we dedicate this
place as home for _____ and _____. Bless
those vagrant, personal things of taste and choice that
put the mark of these particular people upon it and
make it theirs. May it be a place of shelter and protection, of rest and healing, of warmth and hospitality.
And may thy embracing love be seen and felt in all the
celebrations, daily chores, hard decisions, and shared
glories that will occur here. As it will become the store-
house of blessed memories, make it also a place for
growth in grace. We pray in the name of him who has
prepared a place for us, in whose house are many
mansions, even Jesus Christ our Lord. Amen.

On the Birth of a Child

Gracious God, in whom all things have their beginning, and in whom we find our own true end: we give
thanks for the safe birth of your new servant
_____ and for the joy he (she) has brought to
his (her) family. We give you thanks for the hope and
promise and protection with which his (her) life is
surrounded now. And we take with joy that reminder
of the grace that has attended each of us from our
beginning until now. As we give thanks for his (her)
birth, receive as well our thanks for the promise of new
birth given to all in Jesus Christ. Help us to trust in
you and enjoy your presence as we acknowledge with
wonder the perpetual novelty of your love. Amen.

Table Graces

For this food, O Lord, and for all thy blessings, known and unknown, remembered and forgotten, we give thee thanks. Amen.

* * *

We praise thee, Lord, that we have bread to break and love to share and blessings to remember with thanksgiving. Amen.

* * *

Bless the Lord, O my soul, and all that is within me, bless his holy name! For he has given us the kindly fruits of the earth to sustain us and the gift of love to renew us, through Jesus Christ our Lord. Amen.

* * *

Recall to us the hungry, O God, so that we learn thankful hearts for the blessing in this bread. Amen.

* * *

Visit our table with grace, Lord Jesus, and share with us our lives, for we thank thee now for this food and every common blessing. Amen.

* * *

Receive our thanks, heavenly Father, for all thy blessings—this food, this fellowship, our time together—and make us mindful of all who lack such daily gifts. Amen.

O Lord of the living and the dead, the mantle of whose mercy is cast over all things so that nothing in all creation can separate us from your love which we have known in Jesus Christ our Lord: hear our prayers for all who fear death and whose lives are lived in that shadow. Quicken in them a lively hope and a free engagement in this life, its joys and sorrows, its tasks and rewards. May your perfect love come clear to them and cast out fear, as you have promised through your Son, Jesus Christ, in whose name we pray. Amen.

* * *

Hear our prayer, O God, who created us with glory and honor, and who has called us to live in freedom. We give thanks for your servant _____ and for that certain holy ambition that inhabited him (her) and flowed out into the excellence and devotion of his (her) work. By such as he (she), we have had our sense of the world enhanced. Gracious God, be 'our strength and our joy, that we too may apply ourselves to excellence in whatever we do, and by the refining of our gestures of work and play may capture something more of the promise of our humanity. We pray in the name of him who was among us to reveal us to ourselves and assure us of your love, even Jesus Christ. Amen.

For the Bereaved

Gracious heavenly Father, hear our prayers for all who are bereaved by the loss of a loved one. Grant the light of thy presence and thy supporting love to them, O Lord, that their dark moments be not without some light, and their burdens be not intolerable. Strengthen our solidarity with them, both in compassion and in service, and make us instruments of thy tender pity for them and for all sufferers. We pray in the name of Jesus Christ, who promised that the mourners shall be comforted. Amen.

On the Death of a Young Person

O Lord, hear our prayer for your servant _____ who died in the midst of life, his (her) promise still blossoming. Be his (her) comfort and his (her) solace, we pray, and let him (her) rest in your care, where all tears are wiped away and no torment touches. We pray for his (her) family and friends as well, good Lord. Grant them the assurance of faith even when faith in any goodness is severely challenged. Hear their sighs of sorrow, and comfort them. May no bitterness overtake them, nor an end of hope for their own lives. "Blessed are those who mourn, for they shall be comforted." So said our Lord; may it be so for them. Amen.

O God, from whose first fire came the light which dispelled primeval darkness and gave creation its birth; the pillar of whose fire led your captive people, Israel, from slavery into freedom; whose tongues of fire burned away a confusion of tongues and left one new people, the church, aglow with your Spirit: be present again in power to this congregation and their pastor. Grant them energy fit for the works of new creation in their life as a church and in their witness to this community. Endow them with such a holy vision that they will press always toward the promised land of freedom for all oppressed peoples. Enliven them with such faith in your immediate presence that they will speak the prayers and do the deeds that befit a newborn church.

We give thanks that pastor and people have covenanted together this day and have agreed to make their spiritual way supporting each other and ministering to each other. Grant to your servant _____ such understanding and faithfulness that he (she) may rightly divide the Word of truth and administer the sacraments of your grace in a fashion that will nourish the people with the very bread of life, even Jesus Christ our Lord. And grant to this congregation such commitment to their vocation as Christians that they will uphold their pastor as Aaron held the arms of Moses, and fulfill their calling to be a leaven in the growth and a light upon the path of the people of this neighborhood.

We offer our prayers, as we can and as we may, in the name and power of Jesus Christ our Lord. Amen.

Installation of Church Officers

Lord, who desires of thy church that we become a servant people and gladly give ourselves to others: consecrate to thy bold intention these officers (deacons, trustees, committee members) whom we have called in thy name, that faithfully and with a quick responsibility they will perform the duties of their office for the sake of all of us and to thy glory. May thy Spirit guide them with true counsel, keep them tolerant of human frailty, and support them when the rough places are not plain. Cause them to expect that new light shall yet break forth from thy holy Word. Bless them to us and us to them and all of us to thee in a covenant of mutual and joyous ministry to which we are led by Jesus Christ our Lord. Amen.

For Church-School Teachers

Lord of all the little children everywhere, we rejoice on this day that brings us here to praise thee in song and prayers. Especially we give thanks for the teachers who, standing before us, offer themselves unselfishly and gladly that our children hear of thy presence among us, know that thy right hand upholds us, and come to care that thy love makes all life holy and good. Bless these teachers with a rich and redeeming joy in the weeks ahead. Let them carry into this gift of time and imagination our warm thanks and, even more, thy divine approval. Amen.

A Church Anniversary

In this time of remembrance we come, O God, as the
generations before us, to seek thy blessing and to speak
thy praise. We give thanks for those who built this
church by faith, for those who brought to it their
hearts' anguish and their souls' rejoicing, for those who
sang in it to thy glory and those who prayed in it for
the sake of others, and for all that teeming life within
it whereby we have learned and dreamed and hoped
together. Now as we share this bread that hallows and
this cup that saves, be in us a hope and a jubilance for
all the days and years that lie ahead. Praise be to thy
name in this sanctuary forever and ever! Amen.

Dedication of a Church

Come, sovereign Lord, to this time of our jubilation
and so deepen us down in the vows of our faith that
this house which we have built for the uses of thy glory
will become, for all who declare thy praises, a gathering place; for all who wait upon thy word, a listening
place; for all who have need of thy mercies, a healing
place. In all seasons assemble within it the people who
have made a covenant with thee by love, and draw
unto it the lonely and the brokenhearted, the lost and
the afraid, all who have need of sanctuary and hope.
Send forth from this church ministries wrought in thy
holy fire to consume the world's miseries and injustice
and to give such light that many shall desire again the
city of God and make the blessed resurrection their
watchword. Amen.

Service of Music

O Lord our God, who sets thy creation singing wherever it is touched by thy grace: we give thee thanks for the songs and sounds which tie generation to generation. Through the artistry of those who compose and those who perform thou has shaped the language which opens to us that past and overcomes the loneliness of our time in history. We yield our thanks for this and all thy blessings, known and unknown, remembered and forgotten; through Jesus Christ our Lord. Amen.

For a Meeting of the Church

Almighty God, who assembles us here to use ourselves wisely and freely to extend thy purposes for good in this neighborhood and wherever human hearts have need of thee: we beseech thee to brood in our deliberations, to keep spacious and kind our trust of one another, and to cause us to see visions and dream dreams that thy holy will be accomplished among us. Give us judgments weighted by the claims of thy truth upon us and actions that bespeak the imaginations of heaven itself. Urge us always to desire with a full desire to stand against the dark powers in our time, and ready us to declare by our works thy compassionate promises to all generations; through the Lord Jesus, our hope, our pardon, and our peace. Amen.

For the Jews at Passover

Lord God, we pray for our brothers and sisters, the Jews, at their holy season of remembrance of that time when, following your cloud of presence by day and the fire by night, they passed over from exile into freedom. We ask that their acts of recollection will be a source of strength and of faith in your unending care for them and for all your children. Help us, O God of Abraham, Isaac, and Jacob, to commit ourselves to insuring that no winds of holocaust will again blow across Israel, withering and destroying. Make us instruments of your peace, we pray, and hasten the day when the ancient vision of *shalom,* the kingdom of righteousness and peace, will be established in the hearts and communities of all people. Amen.

Days of Awe and Atonement

O God of Abraham, Isaac, and Jacob, who opened to all nations the power of your love through this scattered people, the Jews: grant us thankful hearts for the ties that bind Jews and Christians together as children of the same parents in faith. Now, in the days of Awe and Atonement, O Lord, help us to seek atonement for all the suffering heaped upon Jews by their spiritual kin, the Christians. As children of the same God and heirs of the same promises, we pray now to be forgiven for all those ways we may have sharpened our separation and to be strengthened in all the things that will bring us closer to each other and to you. Amen.

An Ecumenical Occasion

O our one Lord, who calls forth one faith and names us all in one baptism: we pray for the one, holy, catholic, and apostolic church—for Catholic and Protestant, orthodox and unorthodox, evangelical and liberal believers who in their several ways give testimony to Jesus, the author and finisher of our faith. As we share one Teacher and Savior, let us share one spirit and purpose as well, so that the new humanity you are bringing to light will be seen in our common praise and our steadfast love. We pray in the name and for the sake of Jesus Christ. Amen.

For the Whole Church

O Lord our God, who fashioned the church from a scattered band of disciples and gave it power to endure: we pray now for that same moving band of uncertain but hopeful people, the holy catholic church in all its branches. We ask that it be grafted anew to your will for this world and for our time within it. May this fellowship be free enough to live for the world, not just in the world. May it become a sign of your kingdom of justice, peace, and love. Quicken its life, we pray, so that men and women everywhere may look upon it and, seeing its vitality and purpose, come to understand better their own and common destiny; through Jesus Christ our Lord. Amen.

PRAYERS FOR SPECIAL
NEEDS AND PERSONS

For a Spirit of Thanksgiving

Gracious Lord God, from whom we have all the blessings of this life—our daily bread, the love of friends, comforts, challenges, good work and zeal to do it, the shouts of children, the wisdom of elders, the power of healing in our bodies, the capability of growth in our minds, and chief of all thy blessings, thine own love made unmistakable in thy Son: hear us as we praise thy name and offer thanks to thee for all these blessings, as well as for the number of those which are so close to us that we do not think of them. Help us, we pray, to thank thee daily and so to grow in a spirit of thankfulness that we become daily more able to rejoice in thy blessings. Amen.

* * *

Gracious God, when things go badly we invoke your name and implore your help, knowing we are at the boundaries of our own strength. Help us also to call upon your name when all things go well and, by the giving of our thanks, to remember your gracious care for us and for all people. So by our thanksgiving preserve us from thinking that we redeem ourselves. We pray in the name of our only Redeemer, Jesus Christ. Amen.

For the Nation

Come, sovereign Lord, to all occasions of prayer and praise for our country. Keep our celebrations honest as we recall the past, compassionate as we judge the present, and lively as we engage the future. Set loose in the land the wild and wonderful airs of open discussion, dissent, difference, ideas old and new. And in all things uphold us as a people bound to one another and to thee by trust that arises out of high purposes and love that flourishes in shared dreams; through Christ our Lord. Amen.

* * *

O God, whose mercy is over all the nations: go with us now into the uncertainty and the promise of the years that lie before all of us. Turn the hearts of this people away from the uses of force, the illusions of wealth, the contagion of prejudice, and the rule of selfishness. Make us a servant people, following the way of our Lord Jesus Christ. Persuade the nation to lose its life that it may find its soul, and open us to all the weathers of the world that we may learn again to love all people. Amen.

For Those in Authority

Sovereign God, we pray for all those in positions of authority. Give them a new range of vision fit for their estate, a new courage to call forth the highest rather than the meagerest loyalties of those they lead, and a new spirit of self-transcendence that they may withstand the temptation to measure their actions by selfish benefit. And help each of us, in our covenant with them, to support their best desire to serve the common good. Amen.

In Time of War

Gracious God, who has commanded us to love our enemies: grant that in this absurd world so absurd a command will be disregarded no longer. As you have justified us all by your love and have no need to hear us justify ourselves, grant us resolve to press the claims of peace first upon ourselves, and then upon those whom we have wronged and who have wronged us. O Lord, before the momentum of hatred passes our power to control it, grant us peace and a time of rebuilding. Amen.

For Peace

Most merciful Lord, in whose kingdom lion and lamb lie down together: grant to the nations peace and a desire to preserve the same. Give those in authority patience in negotiation and a largeness of spirit to seek true justice through accords. And so touch the minds and hearts of us all that we may be free of hatred and misunderstanding. So may peace be left with us, your peace be given us. Amen.

* * *

O God the Father of the Prince of Peace, look with patience as well as judgment on those who, in all earnestness, nonetheless feed the fires of war. Let nothing hide from us the terror, the tragedy, the despair of war, nor let our honorable motives cover the blasphemy against thy love in every injury and every death visited upon men, women, and children in the name of high principle. O Lord, may we be servants of your peace, not only by our opinions but also by our actions; through Jesus Christ our Lord, who took upon himself our violence that we might have peace in our hearts and in our communities. Amen.

In Time of Racial Strife

Gracious Lord God, whose justice cannot be turned aside and whose peace will prevail at last: grant us both justice and peace in the racial strife that besets us. We pray for the gifts of a calm spirit and a clear mind for all those caught in the midst of the drama, and especially for those who face each other across the borderline of custom and change. Keep the tension from issuing in tragedy, and so guide thy people by thy Holy Spirit that our present afflictions will soon pass and a new era of dignity and opportunity be established for all. Amen.

For Racial Justice

Grant us, O God of many splendors, so to learn from and be encouraged by your Son that we will be servants of your love in all things. Help us to stand more firmly for justice and reconciliation among the races of the earth, and not in opinion only, but also in action and commitment. Grant us such compassion that we may see in the disadvantage of those who suffer discrimination in jobs or homes, schools or courts, that their wounds are ours also, since we are one flesh in Christ. And strengthen us to seek the healing of their circumstance with the same constancy we see in your Son, who suffered freely for our healing. Amen.

For Neighbor-Love

O Lord God, we praise your name for all the rich variety that is found in the human family, your children. We thank you for the different songs by which we sing our joys and sorrows to one another, for the different languages in which we speak our hopes and hungers, for the contrasts of color and stature and sex which catch our eye and make us want to know each other. Glory be to you for the many faces and voices of our family! Now teach us to treasure our differences, great God, as evidence of the endless richness of your love for this world. We pray in the name of our Lord, the Jew who praised a Samaritan; who interceded for an adulteress; who ministered alike to Jew and Gentile, slave and free, men and women, and was not afraid of the wealth of your love. Amen.

For Hope

God of hope and God of glory, may the vision of a new Jerusalem infect us and move us to begin its building in our own lives and in our own society. Make us firm and clear against all arguments from despair—that our enemies are less than human, that the poor are poor because they are lazy, that military force is the only language nations understand, that all other leopards will never change their spots. Grant us, Lord God, a deep understanding that we were not born to die but to begin, to interrupt the flow of despair, to start something new for love's sake. We pray in the name of him who came to make all things new, even Jesus Christ our Lord. Amen.

For the Church

O God, who has set us in the world as an ensign people: we pray for the church and for its witness to your covenant with all peoples. Grant that having acknowledged ourselves as bound into her body, we may take part in her task of being handmaid to divine grace. Teach us to speak the truth in love with our neighbors, to honor all things excellent, to bear our responsibilities with integrity, and to enter into the sufferings of others. So may the knowledge of your healing love be set forth in our lives, and through us your church be renewed. Amen.

* * *

O Lord our God, who has spoken your word with power in the person of Jesus Christ: grant to your church the power to speak your word faithfully through its life as well as its doctrine. Let it be your instrument of holy discontent wherever the world is shoddy, unjust, or calloused against your mercy. Make of it a herald of your kingdom, speaking from the authority of your promise that your word, having gone forth with power, will not return to you empty. May your church be a haven for the lonely, a fortress for the oppressed, and a servant at all times both of your truth and of your covenant; through Jesus Christ, the rock on which we stand redeemed. Amen.

For a Good Witness

Gracious God, we pray that the good news of thy gospel may prosper in us and through us. Grant us freedom from all anxieties, and especially from those in which we confuse personal uncertainties with religious doubts. Release us from all false occupation with ourselves, from all graceless response to others, from all disregard of serious questions, from all need to prove others wrong to show ourselves right. Grant us increasing maturity in outlook and action, so there may be space for thy serenity and thy vigor to control us more and more. Keep us in a quiet mind, in a willingness to be prompted by thee, in a confidence that rests on thy promise. Thus may we bear, without self-consciousness, a good witness to thy gospel for which we daily give thee thanks. Amen.

For Renewed Dedication

Lord Jesus Christ, we pray for a new vision of your love and a new dedication to your will in our daily life. Grant that we may have no lower estimate of humanity than you showed by your passion on the cross; and seeing anew how precious is the life you created in us, grant us the courage to measure ourselves by the stature you have given us. May we never feebly concede to cynicism or despair. Keep alive in us such spiritual courage that our eyes may not wander from the cross, though all about us brood on the prospect of an empty heaven and a soulless humanity. And grant, O Lord, that we will not think ourselves more virtuous than we are, neither imagine ourselves less precious than you have regarded us. Amen.

For Family Life

O God, who has brought us into life by your creating power, and sustained us by your love: hear our thanks for the bonds of family life. We confess that we have sometimes been a trial to each other as we have been to you. Yet we worry one another because we love one another, just as your love for us has been laced with pain. Grant us joy and delight in the knowledge that we have our families, that the roots sprung in childhood will nourish us our life long, and that whether near each other or far apart we will carry within us the confidence that comes from strong loyalties and deep loves. We pray in the name of him who addressed divine majesty with a family name and called you Father, even Jesus Christ our Lord. Amen.

Thanksgiving for Family Life

Thou Parent of our first parents: receive our thanks for the supports of family life. As you have made your own love known through the image of a family in joyous Bethlehem and a larger family at tragic Golgotha, so we remember your love and lean on it in moments of celebration and moments of trial. Keep our minds and hearts alive to the manifold ways you minister to our needs through the family bond, in which you have created and nurtured us, admonished and comforted us, as you did your own Son, in whose name we pray. Amen.

For the Families of the Church

O God, our God, who has fathered us in the rejoicings of heaven and mothered us with affections from the womb of time itself: we hold before thee all those dear to us, near or far away, who have need of thy mercy and thy strength. Keep alive in our families the touch of hands, the hospitalities of love, the festivals of praise, the hopes and memories of all generations, the exchange of peace. And so fill our homes with trust that our windows open on the world and our doors fling wide to minister to the lonely and the stranger. As we are thy family, help us to be family to one another. Amen.

A General Intercession

O Creator Lord, who wills wholeness of spirit and health of body for all your children: hear us, we pray, as we offer intercession for all who stand in special need of your blessing. For those who are chronically ill, to whom no hope of bodily strength can be given—bless them with your presence and the strength of spirit to rise above their reasons for despair into a higher hope; for all who seek in earnest and do not find you—teach them to see your hand in the common things around them, and your face in the face of Jesus Christ; for all who lack food and shelter—may our daily comforts chafe us and move us to share more and more; for those whose special needs we know (whom we recall in our hearts before you _____). Visit them as they have need; through the ministry of Jesus Christ our Lord. Amen.

For the Special Persons

We pray, O most compassionate God, for the little, broken boys and girls, gargoyled and bent in body, humpbacked and slow in mind, and for the old ones numbed and waiting and lost—the special children we have forgotten, the ones kept away from our normal eyes and our comfortable pews. Before their need we repent us our self-pity, our complaint, our luxury. O in thy mercy give us the courage to love these exiled brothers and sisters, and put praise in our hearts for those among us who take these strange and different people in our arms and hold them and rock them into grace, after the example of the Lord Jesus who came to heal and to bring hope. Amen.

For One in Dire Extremity

Merciful God, though we mumble or are struck by a great silence, receive our prayer for thy servant _____ who is sick unto death and in pain beyond endurance. In all that he (she) may suffer be thou round about him (her) as a strength to withstand the shattering hours, as protector against the terror in the night, as companion in all the dark passages. Give to us who watch and wait the deep consolation of thy love, and according to thy promises take unto thyself this thy son (daughter); through Jesus Christ who healeth all our diseases. Amen.

For Those Who Suffer

Before the throne of thy grace, O Lord, we would lay the cares of our fellows. To all those who are bereaved of their loved ones, give the assurance of thy victory over death; to those who suffer from incurable diseases, grant such love of thee as will free their minds and spirits of the bonds of self-pity; to those who endure life under tyranny, grant the dream of freedom and a zeal to pursue it, even at a cost; to those who find no meaning in their lives, grant such self-knowledge and knowledge of thee as may dispel the mists of despair. We ask these boons in the name of Christ, in whom thou hast promised us every grace. Amen.

For the Sick

Merciful God, who has borne the suffering of your children and who stands with us, whether hidden or revealed, when our time of suffering comes: be with all those who are sick in body, mind, or heart, and especially those known to us (whom we remember in our hearts before thee _____). Grant them healing, and where there cannot be healing grant them strength to bear their burdens in the confidence of your never failing love; this we pray in the name of Jesus, our great Physician. Amen.

For the Lonely

We pray especially at this time, dear Lord, for all those who, by reason of sickness or circumstance, feel themselves separated from the love and care of the people around them; or who, by reason of doubt and desperation, know the lonely exile of hours and days empty of hope. By holy mysteries we cannot name let thy healing presence brood among them so that they find again, and with a certainty, that thou art for all of us healer and true companion, sustainer and comforter. Overcome their anxieties with that compassion which causes the lame to walk and the blind to see, even the love of our Lord Jesus Christ. Amen.

At a Parting

O Lord of our common life, who preserves the bonds of understanding and affection we have with one another, we pray for each other and for the community between us. Especially now, as we take leave for a time, do we pray for each other's safety and welfare. Bring us together again, we pray, our community unbroken by tragedy or death; and through all times, whether together or apart, bind us to one another by our common love for you and your Son Jesus Christ, in whose name we pray. Amen.

For the Unemployed

Creator God, who has given us the gifts both of work and of rest: we pray for the unemployed, for whom the want of work is not rest but anxiety. May their plight be continually on our hearts, and our minds be turned to find for them new tasks and opportunities. Preserve us, O God, from equating our own happy industry with virtue, and their enforced idleness with vice. And lead us toward the day when all will have needed work and the sense of dignity it brings; through Jesus Christ our Lord, who has called us to labor together in his vineyard. Amen.

For the Unfulfilled

O God our Creator, who knows our nature and our needs, and has called us to a new estate in Christ, where all our work is praise and service: hear us as we pray for those who have no work to do. Keep them from despair and help them to find the place where their hand can be useful and their self-esteem restored. We pray for all who take no joy in the work they have been given to do, whose days are a drudgery and whose spirits are wearied. We pray too for those who know their work only as the way to private gain. Teach them how to take joy in serving as you have joyfully served both them and us in Jesus Christ. For all of us, may our work become a place of sharing and a time of praise. Amen.

For the Poor

Heavenly Lord, whose Son was among the meek of the earth and called them blessed, who took as his own the burden of poverty and deprivation: grant us, and all who by thy blessing are cast among the rich and powerful peoples of the world, to recall thy poverty, to make common cause with the wretched of the earth, and so to use what we have that we keep our sensibility for others' needs. Lord God, thou hast granted us a share in the glories and joys of this world. Help us, we pray, to become instruments of others' enjoyment of the same; through Jesus Christ our Lord, who came among us that we all might have life and have it abundantly. Amen.

For People in Poor Nations

O Lord, who cares for all, and who gives us liberty to pray for those whose needs we know: we pray for those who live on lands unable to support them decently. Perfect in them and in us that spirit of mutual respect and common concern which can yield a more perfect division of the world's blessings, to the benefit and joy of all, and to the end of a more perfect harmony among the peoples. Amen.

For the Hungry

Lord God of all creation, we pray for the hungry, those a world away and those in our own cities and rural slums whose suffering accuses us and denies the provision you have made for us all in this ample world. Constrain us in our use of the world's goods, we pray, and give us new wills and new ways to reach out toward those who need us. We pray through him who is the living bread which came down from heaven, even Jesus Christ our Lord. Amen.

* * *

Lord God, we confess that we take our table for granted. Hear us as we pray for those whose tables are empty, who have no joy in gathering there. We confess that hungry nations reach out for a loaf and we hand them a gun. O generous God, we cannot pray for the hungry of this world without first praying for ourselves. Grant us determination to change the selfish drift of things, to call upon one another for sacrifice, so that no neighbors anywhere will be given a stone when they need bread; through Christ our Lord. Amen.

For Refugees

Lord God, we pray for all the bombed out, burned out, driven out, relocated, wondering, wandering, unwilling pilgrims in this world. Forgive us for our part in uprooting them. Restore their lives, renew our commitment, and make us partners with them in the rebuilding of their farms and cities, their homes and lives. We pray in the name of the Son of man, who had no place to lay his head. Amen.

For Stewardship of the Earth

O Lord God of all creation, who made this world a garden and appointed us its stewards: help us so to care for your earth that it may produce good fruit and plenty. Keep us from preoccupation with convenience and our own gain, so that we will not despoil this garden and deprive others of its enjoyment. Keep us daily mindful of the hungry, Lord, and of the fact that they need not be so. Let us never forget that we have our abundance at the cost of others' privation. So may we dedicate ourselves to making your earth a place of justice as well as of plenty. We pray in the name of Jesus Christ, in whose name we are commanded to break bread with all. Amen.

For a Larger View of Life

O God of light and love, who calls your children to return from their mad strife and love one another as you have loved them: grant us both to hear and to heed that call, to set aside the enmities that eat at our souls, and to give our whole selves into your hands and thus into love. Through our prayer and praise grant us a new heart fit to adore your glory and able to overcome both great trials and petty annoyances. Thus may we come to that larger view of life in which we will be free of hatred and strong to walk in the way of your love; through Jesus Christ our Lord. Amen.

For True Prayer

When we turn toward you, O God, we confess that it has often been in habit or in desperation, only rarely in adoration or thanksgiving. Hear us now as we bring you our prayers with thanks for your never-ending patience, for your promise to hear us whenever we pray with honest intent. Grant us, then, not many words but a whole heart, not much praying but true prayer. Amen.

Afterword

Much has been written about prayer, sometimes in great declarations, at other times in becoming humility. Yet it is always understood that whatever is said about prayer is not the same as praying; and it may be that those who speak most eloquently on the theme of prayer are not themselves especially prayerful people —a curious paradox. Someone has said that prayer is our meeting place with God. If this is true for us, then at the very least in prayer we have a chance to encounter the deep heavens, to let our very skin feel something of the majesty and compassion of God. I suspect also that prayer is our acknowledgment of our human frailty. It comes upon us when circumstance forces us to acknowledge that we are not finally in charge either of our own lives or of the world that surrounds us. Thus prayer chastens us—a very good thing in itself. If we pray for others, and we sometimes do, prayer opens us to the hurts and frustrations other people know, and perhaps we are taught mercy and forgiveness. It may be that the best prayer is a person's life—how that life continues toward the grace of God day by day.

ARNOLD KENSETH

ARNOLD KENSETH, English teacher, poet, and liturgical specialist, is pastor of South Congregational Church, Amherst, Massachusetts. A graduate of Bates College and Harvard Divinity School, with an M.A. in English from Harvard University, he has taught American Studies at Amherst College and English and Modern Poetry at the University of Massachusetts, and has served as a literary consultant to the National Commission on Worship of the United Church of Christ. His poetry has been published in a host of journals, various anthologies, and four of his own books: *A Cycle of Praise; The Holy Merriment; Poems of Protest, Old and New;* and *Sabbaths, Sacraments, and Seasons.*

RICHARD P. UNSWORTH is Chaplain and Professor in Religion at Smith College. A graduate of Princeton University and Yale Divinity School, with a Th.M. from Harvard University, he has served as Assistant Chaplain at Yale University and as Dean of the William Jewett Tucker Foundation at Dartmouth College. He has prepared study documents in the area of sexuality for the United Presbyterian Church in the United States of America and is a coauthor of *Sex Education and the Schools.*